THE ONLY WAY TO LIVE

RAMESH S. BALSEKAR

YogiImpressions®
THE ONLY WAY TO LIVE
First published in India in 2006 by
Yogi Impressions Books Pvt. Ltd.
1711, Centre 1, World Trade Centre,
Cuffe Parade, Mumbai 400 005, India.
Website: www.yogiimpressions.com

First Edition, September 2006
First reprint[5] – January 2012

Copyright © 2006 by Ramesh S. Balsekar

All rights reserved. This book may not be reproduced in whole or in part, or transmitted in any form, without written permission from the publisher, except by a reviewer who may quote brief passages in a review; nor may any part of this book be reproduced, stored in a retrieval system, or transmitted in any form or by any means electronic, mechanical, photocopying, recording, or other, without written permission from the publisher.

ISBN 978-81-88479-75-7

Printed at: Repro India Ltd., Mumbai

Dedicated to
all the visitors
who have
blessed my home
at the satsangs.

As if...

One morning, a man received a letter stating that he had inherited an old, dilapidated mansion on the outskirts of the city where he lived. His uncle, who had recently passed away, had willed it to him.

On the following Sunday, the man decided to visit this mansion. After inspecting the various rooms, he went up to explore the attic. It was crammed with broken furniture, old rugs, and other odds and ends. Under a heavy, dust-covered rug, he discovered an old wooden chest with a heavy lock. His heart started pounding with excitement, as his mind conjured up all sorts of visions of the valuables locked inside the chest. With shaking hands, he grabbed a spanner and broke open the lock. To his amazement, the chest was filled with bundles of old currency notes. Finding a worn-out suitcase in a corner of the attic, he quickly transferred all the money into it.

The next morning, thinking that it would be safer to keep it in his bank, he took the money to deposit in to his account. Going straight into the Bank Manager's cabin, he told him about his good fortune as he kept piling bundle upon bundle of notes on the desk. The Bank Manager, a wise and cautious man, requested him to wait while he took the money to the Teller to be counted and credited to his account.

The minutes ticked by. The man paced back and forth impatiently in the Manager's cabin. Finally, after what seemed like hours, the Bank Manager returned with a grave and sullen look on his face. The currency notes, he informed him, were counterfeit. Each one was a fake!

So, did the man really have the bundles of currency notes?
Yes, he did.
What was their value? Nothing!
Similarly, does an individual have free will? Yes, he does indeed.
Yet, what is its value? Nothing!
Why?

Because all one can do, in any situation, is to decide to do what one thinks one should do. That's total free will. After that, whatever happens is never in one's control. One of three things can then happen:

1. One gets what one has wanted.
2. One does not get what one has wanted.
3. One gets something totally unexpected, for better or for worse.

Which one of the three things happens is entirely a matter of one's destiny, God's Will or the Cosmic Law.

"Therefore, how should I live my life? By acting as if I have free will, but knowing fully well that whatever happens thereafter is not 'my' will but God's Will."

CONTENTS

Editor's Note | ix
Introduction | 1

BASIC PRINCIPLES OF LIFE AND LIVING

Life Happens | 7
What is the Ego? | 11
Genes and Conditioning | 16
The Value of Free Will | 21
The Working of the Mind | 25
Awareness | 31

DAILY LIVING

Happiness | 39
Relationships | 43
Love | 46
Man and Woman | 48
Loneliness in Daily Living | 50
Criticism | 53
Conflict | 55
Revaluation of Values | 58
Pursuit of Pleasure | 61

Process of Thinking	66
Spontaneity	71
Self-control through Discipline?	74
Fear	76
Self-image and Imagination	81
Knowing Oneself	83
Desire	86
Self-improvement	89
Aspects of Time	92
Free Will and Effort	96
Activity	99
Work	102
Success and Failure	105
Order	108
Good and Evil	115
Meditation	119
Dispassion	125
Spiritual Seeking	127
God and Religion	130
Death	137

LIVE LIKE GOD

The Only Way to Live	143
The Right Attitude to Life	147
Krishna Speaks	153
The One Essence	160
The Final Prayer	167
Afterword	169

EDITOR'S NOTE

For several years now, I have had the privilege to visit Ramesh in Mumbai and enjoy his precise, humorous, kind, and patient way of talking to seekers, who come to him from all over the world.

In his teaching, Ramesh has adopted a down-to-earth approach. In his talks, as well as in the present book, he urges his visitors and readers to seriously ponder over what a human being wants most in life. Furthermore, he challenges the spiritual seeker to question what enlightenment can give a person, what he or she didn't have before. And the answer to both questions is simple: it is inner peace. What everyone truly seeks, irrespective of the means one utilizes or the situations one is confronted with, is inner peace in daily life and living.

For that reason, the impact of his teaching is not lost when one walks out of the 'spiritual door' to deal with the 'other real life' – the teaching and its effects become part of daily living.

From my own experience, Ramesh's teaching, and the understanding it produced, gave me a new perspective of, and a new attitude towards, daily life and living – not more, not less.

One of the several positive effects I have experienced, has been the tremendous improvement in efficiency in my everyday work. The new perspective that no one is the doer of any deed, diminished the worrying about success and approval which interfered with, and interrupted, the job at hand.

Ramesh makes it clear that the difference between the man of understanding and the ordinary man does not lie in the circumstances of life and living – these vary from person to person – but the attitude towards them.

The reader is invited to test the teaching and experience it for him or her self. If you feel challenged or compelled by the simplicity of Ramesh's teaching, this book will have served its purpose.

In the present experience of enjoying life and living.

– Chris Andrelang
Munich, July 2006

INTRODUCTION I

What am I talking about in this book? I am talking about a very simple problem: What does a human being, reasonably comfortable in life, fully aware that life means living from moment to moment, and never knowing whether the next moment will bring pain or pleasure, want most in life?

Happiness? Of course.

Then one must ask oneself: "Why am I not happy all the time?" It is common sense that one cannot expect not to ever have any kind of pain – physical, psychological or financial. With this understanding then, "Why am I unhappy?"

I would urge you to think about this question seriously. If you did you would come to only one simple conclusion:

"I am not always happy because the 'other' will not always do what I want him or her to do. And it is totally impractical to expect the 'other' always to do what I want him to do. Therefore, is it impossible for me to be happy?"

The answer to this apparently unsolvable problem was given by the Buddha 2500 years ago: "Events happen, deeds are done, but there is no individual doer of any deed."

If one was able to accept, totally, that everything is a happening according to God's Will or the Cosmic Law, then there would be no question of blaming anyone for anything – neither 'me' nor the 'other'. The result sounds fantastic: no burden of guilt and shame for 'my' actions, nor any burden of hatred for the 'other' for his actions.

The absence of the load of this guilt and shame, pride and arrogance for one's own actions, and hatred, envy, and malice towards the 'other' for his actions is, itself, the presence or existence of happiness.

If one is able to accept, totally, that everything is a happening according to the Cosmic Law, and that how a happening affects whom – for better or for worse – is also according to the Cosmic Law, then it is clear that no one is responsible for the condition one is in, that, in fact, we are all mere instruments, through which life *happens*.

The only difference between the ordinary man and the man

of understanding is that while the ordinary man believes he has done whatever has been done, the man of understanding knows that free will for the individual entity simply does not exist because everything is predetermined. So, how does the so-called man of understanding – someone who has that total understanding – live his daily life?

The man of understanding lives his everyday life in a simple way: he deals with each situation as it arises, with the total awareness that whatever anyone thinks or does, is precisely according to what God wants him to do. He does whatever he thinks he should do in a given situation (motivation plus free will) with the total acceptance that no one does anything, that everything happens precisely according to God's Will or the Cosmic Law, and therefore, no one need be blamed for anything, neither himself nor the 'other'.

The result is two-fold: firstly, he is constantly at peace with himself and in harmony with the 'other'. Secondly, his mind is always pure, totally free from pride and arrogance for his own 'good' actions, free from guilt and shame for his 'bad' actions, and free from hatred towards anyone for the 'other's' actions. Negative responses like anger or fear may arise and disappear in the moment, but they leave no scar on the mind.

He accepts everything that happens – for better or for worse – as God's Will, and blames no one for any happening –

neither himself nor anyone else. Peace and harmony prevail. Enlightenment or total understanding does not mean an easier life. Life may continue to be difficult, but it certainly becomes simpler and more relaxed.

Every Master has stated that life is a dream, and all human beings are characters within that dream. In that case, how should one live one's life in this apparently real life? The answer is that life and living mean dealing with each situation as it arises, and the only thing anyone can do – and has actually ever done – is to do precisely what one thinks one should do.

BASIC PRINCIPLES
OF LIFE AND LIVING

LIFE HAPPENS |

One of the ordinary man's biggest problems is the question "Why?" 'Why' questions are fundamentally unanswerable because there is no fundamental reason for 'what-is'. Most responses to the "Why?" are not answers to the question but merely how it is that, that is so. "Why am I standing up? Because I am not sitting down." Most questions pertain to what exists in life: "Why does God create dictators who maltreat their people?" "Why does God create handicapped children?" The only answer can be that the basis of the manifestation and its functioning that is called life is *duality*, in which everything exists together with its interconnected opposite or counterpart, and that this applies to every conceivable thing.

There cannot be daily life without male and female, good and bad, beautiful and ugly. Another fundamental principle of 'life' is pleasure one moment, pain the next moment. Yet, without the experience of pain would you ever know what pleasure really is? Pursuing one and avoiding the other means inviting frustration. Not accepting the basic duality of life means *dualism*, always choosing and pursuing one against the other. To set up what one likes against what one does not like is a disease of the mind that leads to constant frustration.

'Life' is obviously the middle between birth and death, and 'living' is the process. But who does the living? "Me, of course," one will answer. But is that truly so? There certainly is the body-mind organism, a three-dimensional object, which grows by itself from childhood through to old age and ultimately death – precisely like a growing plant. But there is apparently no 'me' to live in the plant. The Source has infused in the living being 'life' and an 'ego', which is the identification with the body-mind organism as a separate entity. In the human being has been added something more, which distinguishes him from the animal: the ego has been infused with a powerful sense of personal doership and a new factor called 'intellect', which keeps the human animal asking questions and demanding answers, mainly "Why?"

Is then a 'me' really required for the human body-mind

organism in the natural process from birth to death? The question really boils down to: Is the 'me' really necessary for life and living to happen, or does living happen through the body-mind organism, with the impersonal energy functioning through the organism and producing whatever is supposed to happen according to God's Will or the Cosmic Law?

Is it not a fact of life that everything is a happening through a body-mind organism and not the deed done by an individual entity? Life happens. Whatever we do at any moment is based entirely on two factors, genes and conditioning, over which no individual has ever had any control. It is one's destiny according to God's Will or the Cosmic Law.

The only 'real' answer to all the 'Why' questions is that the one who wants to know does not really exist at all — all there is, is Consciousness. That which asks the question, is really nothing more than a three-dimensional object. And then there is no answer — the problem dissolves.

Life and living means one does whatever one is programmed to do, accepting 'his' action as a happening according to God's Will or the Cosmic Law. And one has to accept the consequences of 'his' or 'her' action as judged by society: good, bad, or indifferent. One's action and society's judgement are both happenings according to God's Will or the Cosmic Law. This is life. This is living. This is the natural order in everyone's life.

Everything, including life itself, happens according to a conceptual Cosmic Law, which applies to the whole universe and for all time – and, therefore, the basis of such a vast and complex law can never be intelligible to the meagre human brain.

What then is the meaning of life? Why should the question arise at all? Is not living, in itself, its own purpose, its own meaning? Only the ordinary man wants more because he is so dissatisfied with his life. His life seems so empty and so monotonous that he looks for something beyond what he is doing. But a man who is living truly richly, who sees things as they are and accepts the 'what-is', is not confused and therefore he does not ask what the purpose and meaning of life is. His life is not empty and, therefore, he has no need to find the purpose of life. Such a 'purpose of life' can only be mere intellection without any reality.

WHAT IS THE EGO? I

The ordinary man will always refer to himself as 'me'. Is that 'me' the truth or merely a concept, a thought? A concept is that which someone would agree with but could be denied by anyone. The truth is that which no one can deny. 'God', for example, is a concept because an atheist is entitled to deny the existence of God. On this basis, the only truth is the impersonal awareness of *being*, of existing. If one's entire memory is wiped out, what remains is the impersonal awareness. "I am" (I exist) can never be denied by anyone.

Yet, is this impersonal awareness of *being* the same as the 'me', which is also referred to as the ego? When one says, "I am afraid," who says it? Who is that entity, that thought, which says "I am afraid?" For instance, when a thought makes the statement, *I am jealous,* that thought, for the time being, considers itself permanent because the thought has recognised a similar feeling which it has had before. What one has had before as an experience is given permanence and continuity through recognition of what is taking place now. In other words, thought has continuity because thought is the response of the bundle of memories which constitute tradition, knowledge, experience – conditioning. The whole bundle is the ego: violence, ignorance, ambition, and greed; it has pain, despair, and so on.

The ego invents time as a means of escape – "I will practice, I will meditate" – hoping, gradually, to escape from the prison. Or, it seeks expansion through identification with God, with a concept, with an ideal, with a formula. All escapes from daily living, including television and other forms of entertainment, are actually an effort to get away from the identification of the 'me' as the doer and experiencer. When one says that the purpose of life is to be happy, to find God, then, surely, that desire to find God is an escape from life, from a life that is devoid of peace and harmony. Change of environment may produce a temporary relaxation but the sense of doership, greed, and envy rears its head very quickly. While watching a movie, for instance, all that happens is that the 'me' gets identified with a character in the movie, and suffers his experience.

In other words, it has become a slave to a space and a time of its own. But, as long as there is an ego, there can be no freedom.

The point is that as long as there is an ego, the observer, the thinker, the doer, whatever he seems to be doing, will necessarily be within the prison walls of the 'me' and the 'other'.

What, then, is the role of the 'me' in daily living? The ego is a creation of the Source or Consciousness to function as an individual entity and create a relationship between the 'me' and the 'other' as the basis of daily living. Consciousness is present in the body-mind organism every split-second, in one form or the other: identified consciousness as the ego in the waking state and the dream state, and impersonal consciousness in the deep sleep state. It is the impersonal energy or consciousness, which produces both the doing and the experiencing in the human organism. In other words, the ego is consciousness: impersonal consciousness, identified with the body-mind organism (and a name) as a separate entity with a sense of personal doership. The animal has an ego-identification with the body as a separate entity – but without the sense of personal doership. But even the man of understanding, with total ultimate understanding, responds when someone calls his name. Therefore, there is, clearly, an acceptance of himself as a separate entity. Then, where is the difference between the man of understanding's ego and the ordinary man's ego? The difference lies entirely in the fact that the ordinary man's ego is full of the sense of personal doership, whereas in the man of understanding's ego, the sense of doership has been totally destroyed.

The real problem is whether it is possible to live fully, completely in this world, doing one's job, doing everything efficiently, *in spite* of the ego. Now, is there a method to get rid of the ego? Methods belong to time and, therefore, will not do, whoever the Master. So, if there is no method, no system, no Master, what can be done?

It is an interesting point that it is the ego *itself* asking this question: "Is it possible for me to live life with a sense of fulfilment, not restricted to this prison of the relationship with the inevitable 'other'?" And, it is the ego which has to arrive at the only solution to this problem. It is the ego that has to find out what actually constitutes the 'prison walls' and if it is supposed to happen, according to its destiny, God's Will, or the Cosmic Law, the ego will, at some point of time, realise, with tremendous intensity, that it is its sense of personal doership, which is the cause of its 'imprisonment', bondage.

Even without the doership, the ego will necessarily continue to be the operational element in daily living, even though it will not be the overall functional element which, in all body-mind organisms, is the impersonal consciousness. The ego will continue to have free will to do whatever is necessary in a situation, though, of course, it will have no control over what happens as actual action; thereafter, the ego will have to accept the decision of society in regard to the action as good or bad, reward or punishment. The reward from society will mean pleasure, and punishment will mean pain, from moment to moment. And this, indeed, will constitute the daily living of the ego's body-mind organism.

But, the fact would remain that, while the pleasure would necessarily be enjoyed and the pain suffered by the individual entity, the ego, having totally accepted that it is not the doer in either case, will be free of both pride and guilt. The absence of both pride and guilt would mean the presence of peace and harmony for the ego.

The total realisation that the 'me', the ego, can never be the doer of any deed leads to enlightenment.

GENES AND CONDITIONING I

What is generally known as one's nature is, in fact, what can be called 'programming', consisting of two factors: genes and conditioning, the latter being one's education in a particular geographical and social environment and one's experience. Whatever one does in any situation is necessarily based on these two factors, over which one has never had any control. One has to accept one's genes and conditioning as they are.

One had no control over being born to particular parents, and therefore, no control over his or her genes. Similarly, one had no control over the geographical environment in which one's parents lived, nor over the social environment of one's parents, in which environment this body-mind organism received its conditioning – conditioning at home, in society, in school, church, or temple. The result has been that whatever one thought and did, at any time, according to one's free will had, necessarily, to be based on these two factors.

The way the body-mind organism reacts to any situation is based on its programming. When the eyes see something, the ears hear something, the nose smells something, the tongue tastes something, or the fingers touch something, the reaction, which is generally considered as that person's reaction is, in fact, the biological reaction in the body-mind organism, based on the genes and the conditioning. In fact, the ego gets involved in the situation only when it reacts to the biological reaction, which happens in the case of the ordinary man.

When, for example, anger arises, the ego reacts to this fact and says, "I am angry," and thus gets involved in the situation. Yet, there should be the understanding that anger is a phenomenon that arises in the mind as a reaction to a happening. No one gets angry with anyone. The man of understanding would witness anger arising in a body-mind organism, which then happens to be his own. He merely witnesses anger arising, taking its course, and then disappearing; there is no involvement. A happening that brings out anger in one body-mind organism may not bring about anger in another organism, another person. In another person, the same happening may arouse compassion. The reaction depends on the way the particular organism has been programmed – genes plus conditioning, over which one has had no control. When this is clearly understood, the reaction that so often causes disharmony in relationships will not happen: either, 'he' has made 'me' angry, or 'he' is angry with 'me'.

In a given situation, the biological reaction in the body-mind organism may produce three different reactions in three persons. Anger may arise in one, fear in another, and compassion in the third. Each reaction would be based entirely on the programming – genes and conditioning – and the ego would have no say in the matter.

Yet, conditioning is also shaping the ego-centre or 'me' and is, therefore, at the root of the ordinary man's problems. Especially by thinking – which is nothing more than reacting to the challenges of life from the mind's store of memories – the ordinary man gives more attention to what was in the past and what will be in the future than to 'what-is'. This causes the division of the mind's content into subject and object, thinker and thought, experiencer and experiencing. Conditioning creates a feeling of separation from fellow-beings, and then provides armour against them. Thus, the ordinary man is prevented from having harmonious relationships.

Conditioning manifests itself in attaching disproportionate

importance to time, that is, to division of experiences into past and future. Instead of dissolving the past and shaping the future in the ever-real present, the ordinary man uses this moment, in which he lives, for carrying his sorry past into a dismal future. This conditioning through past and future is responsible for his worries, repentances, frustrations, regrets, hopes, and ideals, for his unshaken belief in causation, fate, karma, evolution, and heaven, and for his demand for the immortality of endless time. These are all due to the conditioned mind and are entirely unnecessary.

All conditioning is to be found in the 'me' or the ego-centre. When one examines one's psychological memories closely, one finds that they have left a 'scar'. The factual memory of a past event has been distorted by the pleasure or pain experienced at that moment. Thus, conditioning is related to the more obvious problems of life: miseries, sorrows, conflicts, frustrations, worries, and fears. When one realises the extent to which the mind is conditioned by psychological memories, it comes as a shock.

No intellectual discipline or cultivation of virtue can destroy memory. One cannot remember to forget. The only way is to see the fact as it is, to accept the conditioning, and thus not get involved. In other words, one has to realise, totally, that the only thing that works is 'awareness'. When the ordinary man realises that his mind is full of such scars, when he is totally aware, the problem disappears. The prevention and the cure come through awareness, not through trying to 'purify' the mind by special exercises. In other words, to see the conditioning 'as it is', with passive and silent awareness, without condemnation or justification. *The only way is to make the conditioning wither away.*

THE VALUE OF FREE WILL 1

What is daily living but dealing with situations as they arise? Dealing with a situation means to do whatever one thinks one should do, to get whatever one wants in any situation one faces at a particular time. This is precisely what the first man on earth did – he used his free will. It is a fact that, in a given situation, the human being could only always do the same thing – thousands of years ago, today, and thousands of years later – and that is to decide what he wants in that situation (motivation) and the kind of effort he would put in to get what he wants (free will).

The fact of the matter is that it is everybody's personal experience that once one has exercised one's free will in doing whatever one wants, in any situation, what actually happens has never been in one's control:

1. One gets what one has wanted.
2. One does not get what one has wanted.
3. One gets what one has not wanted.

Thereafter, society treats what has happened – one of the three things – as one's action, evaluates it according to its own standards and legal provisions, and either rewards one or punishes one. Reward means pleasure in the moment and punishment means pain in the moment.

One is forced to live in society, and must accept society's judgement. It then becomes a fresh situation and the whole process is repeated. It is an undoubted fact that the very basis of the mechanism of daily living is total free will. But it is also a fact that having done whatever one wanted to do in any situation, the result or consequence has never been in one's control. Whatever actually happens all the time is whatever is supposed to happen according to God's Will or the Cosmic Law.

The human being, indeed, has total free will to do whatever he wants to do in any given situation, but in daily life and living, his free will has no value. It is worthless. This situation is not unlike the situation where a man finds a bundle of currency notes in an old chest in the attic of an ancestral home he has inherited. He is delighted at this unexpected discovery. He goes to the bank the next morning to deposit the large amount in his account, but he is told that the currency is counterfeit and, therefore, useless. However, the fact remains that the man did have a bundle of currency notes. Similarly, although free will turns out to be worthless in practice, the human being has total free will in dealing with any situation.

Yet, free will is counterfeit because, whatever the decision and the deed, it is based entirely on two factors – genes and conditioning – which God made, and over which the human being has absolutely no control. This fact leads to another interesting fact: if what one does at any time is based entirely on two factors which God made, it clearly means that whatever one does at any time is precisely what God expected him to do. Even what certainly appears to be one's free will is actually based on two factors, which God made:

1. One's genes, over which no one has any control.
2. The conditioning at home, in society, one's reading, and one's experience.

Therefore, it is inevitable that what one has done in the circumstances is precisely what God wanted one to do. Whatever may be the consequences of one's action according to God's Will, one could not have made any 'mistake', nor could one have committed any sin. *One's free will cannot be different from God's Will.*

So, where is our 'responsibility'? If everything is a happening according to God's Will or the Cosmic Law and not the 'doing' by any individual entity, how can anyone be blamed for anything, either 'me' or the 'other'? That, subject, of course, to our responsibility to the society, which will judge every action of every individual as good or bad and reward the individual or punish him.

Incredible as it may seem, both one's own will and God's Will prevail in daily living at the same time. A given situation has happened because of God's Will. In that given situation, it is one's own will that prevails. However, what actually happens as a result of one's effort has never been in one's control. It is always God's Will.

If one is prepared to accept, totally, that nothing can happen unless it is supposed to happen according to God's Will, according to the Cosmic Law, whatever the consequences of any action, one will not have to fear any punishment from God. If one need not fear God, nothing prevents one from loving one's Creator.

In other words, everything is predetermined, and the human being can never know what it is that has been predetermined. One can only live one's life witnessing whatever happens, without any judgement, and accepting 'what-is' from moment to moment. This is life and living.

As one ponders over this, one comes to realise that one's 'free will' is a big joke.

THE WORKING OF THE MIND

The ordinary man has a hard time accepting that his free will does not give him any control over the outcome of his decisions, because he is destined to make only partial use of his mind. This is why he feels limited, petty, jealous, addicted to comparisons and competition and creating distinctions between good and bad, intelligent and dull, educated and illiterate, rich and poor, master and servant, thus causing discontent and exploitation, class hatred, and conflict.

The ordinary man's mind – his partial mind – is full of random activities that disturb and worry him. If one took the trouble of keeping track of what is passing through the mind over a period of a few hours, one would be astonished: aimless activities such as cursing lost opportunities, worrying about imaginary losses, being jealous or envious of one's peers, holding imaginary discussions with people one is never going to meet, making imaginary plans that are never going to materialise, having secret ambitions, fears, greed, and harbouring resentments.

The partial mind wants permanence through ideas, concepts, fixed patterns, laws and codes, consistency and continuity. It seeks explanations by the known and familiar and lives in fear of the unknown and the unfamiliar. In consequence, the partial mind is tortured by a sense of emptiness, which it tries to contemplate by identification with possessions, power, and status, and is thus responsible for greed, avarice, and vanity in the world.

In other words, what the partial mind usually does is to recognise and verbalise, and thus divide one's consciousness in different ways. It gets conditioned to 'psychological memories', and it is a fact of life that most problems – individual or social – are only the revival of these memories and the conditioning on which these memories are based.

Only the whole, unconditioned mind is capable of seeing things as they are, without separating them into fragments. Thus, a relationship is an integrally felt fact in the mind, without any separation into fragments. For example, you meet someone and for no obvious or apparent reason your heart is drawn to him or against him. The whole mind, without the sense of space and time, exudes a quiet confidence, with which each situation gets tackled on its merits.

The silence of the unconditioned mind is not the one of sleep or death; it is the silence of effortless harmony, of going willingly with life. The mind freed from disturbances is more efficient than otherwise. Like a rapidly rotating top, apparently still, it is made stable by its own momentum, true to its own axis.

How does the 'whole mind' work?

The partial mind considers 'me' – the thinker, the knower, the experiencer – to be necessary in daily life and living, because without it life would mean a stream of experiences, and the partial mind is frightened of having to float aimlessly in such a stream. The whole mind – without the sense of personal doership – is quite at home with the stream of happenings, living in the dynamic, everlasting, timeless present moment.

The partial mind, being essentially separative, based on the rivalry between 'me' and the 'other', cannot ever truly appreciate cooperation between 'me' and the 'other', let alone love. Love, as the partial mind knows it, resting on 'me' as the pivot, can only be selfish love, however much one tries to disguise it. The whole mind, on the other hand, has totally accepted the concept of non-doership of the individual entity and sees all separate entities as merely separate instruments through which events happen according to the Cosmic Law. The whole mind has thus accepted all separate entities as instruments through which life happens.

The partial mind is time-bound – concerned with the dead past and the illusory future, it neglects the present. The whole mind, on the other hand, is concerned only with the present moment. The conditioned or partial mind is stale, bored, and pursues stimulants while the whole mind sees everything freshly 'as if it were the first sunset it has ever seen', and, therefore, needs no artificial stimulants. The present moment is dynamic but the partial mind tries to stabilise action by splitting it into a number of static states.

The partial mind lives in the known and constantly tries to transform the unknown into the familiar known. It is only the whole mind that can feel the dynamism of the unknown. Every activity of the partial mind causes much waste of energy because it tries to form the 'what-is' into the imaginary 'what-should-be'. The whole, unconditioned mind is only concerned with the present moment – the 'what-is' – and, thus, has vast reserves of energy that can give rise to creativity from moment to moment.

The whole mind knows only 'what-is', whereas the partial

mind, working through the brain and its memory, has created a 'present future' with a high degree of accuracy only insofar as the ponderables are concerned. The partial mind, however, is incapable of handling the imponderables.

The partial mind is in operation when there is a subject-object relationship with its judgements; the whole mind is in operation when there are no judgements and 'what-is' in the moment is accepted. The partial mind, divided into subject and object, reasoning by comparing of opposites, necessarily sees these opposites – all opposites – as different while the whole mind sees the opposites as not different. Subject and object are not different.

When the whole mind works, one is not conscious of any details. As no single detail obtrudes over others, one almost feels it is not working at all. The objects it perceives are not clear-cut, and therefore, one's knowledge – or the feel – cannot be easily communicated by words or symbols as we normally do. Actually, one may be using it more often than one realises. In the present, while it lasts, its feel is unmistakable, but it does not leave any memory behind, and thus cannot be recalled in retrospect. The whole mind is dynamic and cannot be held captive in a state of experience or be amendable to discipline or effort.

But, after examining ourselves thoroughly, through awareness, all this disappears – no memories, no belief, no nationality, no isolation, and no desire to hurt anyone or to recall all the supposed hurts. We begin to see things as they are, remaining with 'what-is', without trying to escape from it, without condemning it or trying to overcome it. The brain becomes merely a recording instrument without horizontal thinking – involvement – using it as the 'me' in operation. And the mind becomes truly quiet, functioning only when necessary. Only this quiet mind has the capacity to respond to the immeasurable. When one is truly aware of what we are doing and its disastrous results, one stops doing it without compulsion, without effort, with the deep and sudden insight of awareness.

'Whole mind' means living like God. 'Partial mind' means living like a human being.

AWARENESS I

The whole mind and its 'passive alertness' are the basis of awareness: its passivity exposes the unreality of the disturbed activities of one's partial mind, and its alertness enables us to catch the intimations of the Real, unconditioned or the whole mind, to receive the finer and more delicate communications from the whole mind to its maximum capacity.

Awareness de-conditions the mind. It dissolves the false ideas and desires arising from non-awareness. The unconditioned mind then feels light and free, silent and peaceful. In the state of awareness the mind is extremely alert, fluid, and sensitive, and is thus able to penetrate into 'what-is', into the nature of things, into the hearts of people.

Awareness of the entire process reveals the possibility of a different way in which the mind could work, a way free from conditioning, free from the limiting habits of comparison and judgement.

The most distinctive characteristic of awareness is that it is free from disturbances. The disturbances belong to the ordinary man's partial mind, which 'wants' to be different from 'what it is'. It is not able to accept 'what-is' and creates an illusory 'what-should-be'. The strength of these disturbances depends on their remaining undetected. In the light of awareness, they are easily laid bare, lose their powers, and then cease to affect us. Then the mind is calm and silent, and open to the Reality, the 'what-is'.

Awareness, in a way, is very similar to the effort of waking up and not falling asleep again. With awareness, one begins to feel that things impress one differently: one finds that people are unique and not all similar, that life is creative, not imitative, that everything is related, not isolated. Such impressions are not merely noticed but are actually experienced in concrete situations, with a more awakened and receptive mind. Thus, the whole attitude to life changes. It becomes harmonious and more meaningful and joyous.

Awareness, a movement of the unconditioned or whole mind, brings in many new factors unknown to, and undetected by, the conditioned mind – factors like freedom from the past, freedom from comparison, and new capacities like understanding creativity, love, and relationships. Awareness, therefore, means observing the whole movement of like and dislike, of the suppressions. But awareness is a happening, not a trick, not something that could be used to help to dissolve the things one does not want.

There is also a gain in sensitivity. Awareness helps us to realise that disturbance and agitation are foreign to the true nature of the mind. It is sensitive to the slightest disturbance, however caused, and rejects it as alien to its nature. In other words, the understanding releases the mind from conditioning and makes it sensitive to 'facts as they are' – 'what-is' – not coloured by preconceptions. It works as a catalyst that activates the whole mind into its lively presence.

The finest and the most obvious intimation we receive is that of its own silence or peace. When intimations of such peace come to us, there is no mistaking their presence or their status. It is a positive and live peace that can hold its own against disturbances not by fighting them, but understanding them. Awareness, thus, not only exposes the unreality of the partial, disturbed mind, but also shows the reality of the whole, peaceful, silent mind.

The unconditioned view is open to unique creativeness,

relationship, and experiencing. The state of awareness gives us a true insight into our minds and makes us accept and be more at home with reality. One has to experiment with the awareness of concrete problems of life. If one takes up some relatively easier problem, such as a passing displeasure, a twinge of jealousy, or a pang of conscience, awareness will dissolve it. But a stronger and more persistent disturbance, such as a deep rooted hatred of a rival or a long-standing worry, will, of course, need a certain amount of persistence and hard work. The important point is that being immediately aware is not a special gift of special people, but is possible for any ordinary person, through understanding.

The question, therefore, is: Can awareness be so intensified that not only would it suggest the presence of the unconditioned Real, but soften and weaken the hold of the conditioned mind, so that the intimations of the whole mind could become the principal guides in daily living?

It is important to remember that pursuing awareness or the unconditioned is a reversal to the conditioned mind and leads to a deeper and more tenacious conditioning. For, pursuing is done by someone who thinks he is in bondage and seeks freedom from that bondage. It is only in full awareness of 'what-is' that the mind gets a chance to turn round, leaving all conditioning behind, and to enter into a new and more meaningful life.

Awareness cannot be willed and secured with effort and struggle. The ordinary man's psychosomatic organism finds it hard to understand and adapt itself to its promptings. One can only trust life to take oneself through. The very choicelessness of awareness – without condemnation, justification, and identification – is, by itself, the greatest protection. Conditioning will wither and vanish only in the clear light of awareness.

Anything else other than awareness will create the same conditioning over and over again.

DAILY LIVING

HAPPINESS I

What is happiness? 'Happiness' is a word that is so commonly used that one has ceased to wonder what it really means in daily living. 'Contentment'? Yes, but the word has so little significance without actual experience. After a great deal of thinking over the matter, and experiencing, one probably cannot help but assume that 'happiness' has really nothing to do with the pleasure that possessions and relationships might bring, however deep it may feel.

Personally, I have come to the conclusion that happiness really means so little – and so much: happiness means not expecting anything from anybody, not wanting anything from anybody. Genuine happiness ultimately turns out to be the absence of unhappiness. Unhappiness consists in not accepting the 'what-is', and creating and pursuing an illusory 'what-should-be'.

The core of happiness in daily living is not the amount of pleasure one expects but the capacity to accept 'what-is', without creating and pursuing an imaginary 'what-should-be'. In a verse in the *Ashtavakra Gita,* Ashtavakra tells his disciple, King Janaka: "If you detach yourself from the identification with the body (as the doer of actions), and remain relaxed in Consciousness, you will, this very moment, be happy, at peace, and free from bondage."

What he, in effect, tells his disciple is that he has wrongly identified himself as the individual doer of all actions that happen through the body-mind organism, and thus assumed the responsibility for all actions. This is the root of unhappiness in daily living: the burden of guilt and shame for one's actions.

What Ashtavakra tells his disciple is to witness all that happens in life as something that has to happen according to God's Will or the Cosmic Law. No one need be blamed for anything. With this deep understanding, one can only do whatever one thinks one should do in a given situation, and thereafter, merely witness whatever happens, but not as one's own action. In other words, one witnesses the flow of life, and therefore, remains relaxed and happy.

But, what the ordinary man wants is to stop the movie of life at a particular 'still' that is then considered to be happiness. The ordinary man does not see change as life itself, just as the flow is really the river. The root of the problem of insecurity in daily living is the fact that one fails to really see that change is an integral aspect of life. The only way to make sense out of change is to join it: either plunge into life and welcome change as the spice of life or resist and set oneself against oneself and be frustrated.

The root of frustration for man is the fact that he lives not in the present moment but for the illusory future, which is only a creation of the mind, a mere influence based on memory, an abstraction at best.

It is obvious that the brain, with its fantastic memory bank, is an absolute necessity in order to live in this world. One cannot, however, ignore the whole mind because that is the basic Universal Consciousness. Human beings need both the brain-thinking and the intuitive wisdom to lead a well-balanced, harmonious life. But, what mankind has done is to allow the brain-thinking to develop so fast that intuitive wisdom has been almost forgotten.

The problem is that man cannot be happy even if the present moment provides him with everything he wants. He must have a future, a secure future. And yet, he knows that the future does not stop with the achievement of any particular goal.

The tragedy of this situation is that he cannot even really enjoy that which is presently available to him in ample measure. Only a true understanding of the whole matter (which would make him a man of understanding) would permit him a total, uninhibited enjoyment of what is available in the present moment.

The man of understanding is able to accept this routine of daily living and is happy. The ordinary man is not able to accept 'what-is', and is 'unhappy'. He wants pleasure but not pain, whereas the duality of pleasure and pain, along with all other dualities, is the very basis of 'life' and its functioning.

True happiness can exist only in a clean and pure mind ('purity' being totally independent of any conceptual morality) that is free of both experiential scars and burdens of expectation; a mind alert enough to be receptive to any communion from the Source. Such happiness is not a momentary experience, but a constant living experience.

The key to the situation is: do whatever you think you should do for the ponderable future, and then stay in the present moment. Therefore, the ultimate prayer would be: *"O Lord, please give me a state of mind in which I shall not want anything at all, not even from You."* According to God's Will or the Cosmic Law, and one's destiny, it can bring about happiness with oneself and in relationships.

RELATIONSHIPS I

Life and living are based on relationships. 'Relationship' is, in fact, the very essence of life and living. Without relationship, there is no existence of 'me' and the 'other', whoever the 'other' may be. Apart from the emotional screen that may be thrown up, the fact is that relationship is based on mutual gratification.

Two qualities are necessary for a harmonious relationship in daily living: humility for oneself and tolerance for the 'other'. The absence of these qualities means disharmony in relationships and unhappiness in general. It is the total acceptance of non-doership, that everything is a happening according to God's Will or the Cosmic Law and not the doing by any individual, which naturally gives rise to these two qualities. They cannot be acquired.

Thus, to take the instance of, say, jealousy in a relationship, the condition exists because the 'me', by its very nature, has been acquisitive, and jealousy was only waiting for a chance to flare up. The conditioned state prevents the human being from seeing the situation integrally as a single event in the present moment.

If one can stand outside the turmoil and watch what is going on without judging the situation with approval or disapproval, one would see the situation in a new light. Direct insight into the 'other's' heart and mind is a peculiar quality of the whole mind. The conditioned mind compares 'its' own possessions with the neighbour's, and envies him his great security and comfort.

The unconditioned mind sees this trap, and the understanding creates a new relationship between me and my neighbour, not as rivals or competitors but as fellow instruments, through which life happens precisely according to God's Will or the Cosmic Law. This is the only foundation for relationships and an integrated and creative social life.

It is for this reason that I request my listeners to "listen totally." They are not listening totally if, while they sit before me, they are comparing their own existing opinions or what they learned from books to what I am expressing. Then obviously there is no relationship.

What I aim to do is certainly not brainwashing. I want my listeners to examine what I say but not at the same time as they are listening to what I say. The fact of the matter is that, during a talk, we are both trying to understand the issue of the problem. For this purpose, the mind has to be free from conflict and both passive and alert, not hooked on any opinion or judgement. Understanding can happen only when there exists the swift pliability of a passive mind.

The basic fact about a real relationship between two people is that there is communion between them. This means there is no isolation; there is love and not responsibility or duty.

Relationship is generally sought where there can be security, a state of gratification, all of which creates conflict, because it results in possession, in condemnation, in self-assertive demands. In that there can be no love.

Therefore, 'relationship' has very little significance when one is merely seeking mutual gratification, but becomes extraordinarily significant if it means self-revelation and self-knowledge. A true relationship between a 'me' and the 'other', whoever the 'other', can only exist when one rids oneself of one's possessions, the most precious of which is one's sense of personal doership. There can be true relationship only when there is love, not the search for gratification. *Love can exist only when there is self-forgetfulness.*

LOVE I

What is love? 'Love' is an astonishingly misconceived word in daily living. The ordinary man cannot really imagine 'love' apart from the desire for possession. Indeed, the desire for possession becomes the touchstone for gauging its sincerity, to such an extent that even a mother is accused of not 'loving' her child in the absence of a prominent attitude of possession.

But one may wonder if 'love' is a sentiment at all. The fact of the matter is that love cannot really be a sentiment or emotion but a state of mind, and what is generally known as 'love' is a violent manifestation of the ego. Indeed, love is truly love in the degree in which the selfish element is transcended. Actually, 'love', the emotional sentiment, and 'love' that is a profound but un-emotive love for a chosen object, are infused by the same force and are basically identical – the one covered in egoistic debris, the other pure.

Love with a motive is not love. Nor is love for any gain or profit love. If someone 'loves' another person because this person has something to give – it is not love, it's a deal. But it is love if one respects another and treats him or her the same way whether he or she has something to give or not.

The state of mind that is genuine love is self-sufficient, has a non-spatial character, and is independent of physical presence or sensual contact: no expectation of anything from the 'other', demanding nothing. Yet, since the relationship is based on 'me' and the 'other', physical expression of love is in no way excluded – it may even be an essential element in the relationship, a culmination, the vital expression. But the point is that, in this case, the ego remains in passive abeyance.

One cannot find love by seeking it. Love cannot be cultivated. Love can only *happen* in a relationship that is based on harmony. And harmony in relationships can happen only with the total acceptance, not merely intellectual acceptance, that life really means a series of happenings, strictly according to God's Will or the Cosmic Law. Therefore, whatever effect a happening has on anyone, no one is to blame. No one need be hated.

MAN AND WOMAN

Love between man and woman is greatly misunderstood in daily living. It is a fact of life that men and women have an urgent need of one another, and yet they rarely, if ever, truly understand one another. Somehow, a state of enmity usually exists between them, and almost unceasing conflict.

On analysis, this conflict will be clearly seen to be nothing other than a struggle for domination. The obstacle that lies between them is two fictitious egos. And the root of the obstacle lies not in the ego itself but in its sense of doership. Without the sense of doership, it is perfectly easy to comprehend that the two separate entities – a male and a female – are made for each other. A harmonious relationship does not really involve, as is generally imagined, any sacrifice on either side, except, of course, the sacrifice of the non-existing doership.

Similarly, when men and women accuse one another of disloyalty, it is usually a question of facts, and on examination, almost every time, 'facts' are found to be false, exaggerated, and often misinterpreted. The secret lies in the spontaneity of love – love and disloyalty can never go together.

The association of the male and female has the apparent effect of restoring the imbalance in each element to a state of equilibrium.

In view of the fact that the attainment of equilibrium is constantly and naturally sought throughout life and living, the mutual attraction of male and female – and the mutual need of one for the other – becomes easily comprehensible. But it is doubtful if this need ever attains fulfilment in life, or whether it only remains in a state of stimulation. In fact, the attraction and conflict between the sexes seems to be present at the same time, most of the time.

The more dynamic and less impermanent instances of this universal process are somewhat inappropriately called 'love', because the ordinary person is not able to conceive of love as apart from the essential desire for possession. Actually, the essence of 'love' is to give to the 'other', not to receive something from the 'other'.

LONELINESS IN DAILY LIVING

It is a fact of life that many human beings are lonely and isolated. It can be seen, quite clearly, that what one usually does is to run away from this loneliness through attachment, which is not love, through activity, or through some form of religious or even worldly entertainment. The fact of the matter is that even in an intimate relationship, the ordinary man always thinks about himself; he is self-centred. Whether the ordinary man works in an office or in a factory, whether he does social work or is concerned with social welfare, the fact of the matter is that his self-preoccupation brings about a sense of isolation.

Relationship is surely the basis of daily living, and it is interesting to enquire into the basis of relationship – what it means to be related. One knows how very vital relationship is in life, and yet there exists, in the usual relationship, a distinct barrier between oneself and the 'other'. Whether the ordinary man likes it or not, it is a fact of life that throughout the period of any relationship, an image has been created of the 'other' and, thus, it so happens that the relationship is usually not between two individuals but between two images, formed by each of the other. It is for this reason that in a close relationship, even of many years, there is usually, deep down, a feeling of isolation. The real point, therefore, is whether it is possible to live one's life without the images of one another. It is also clear that one cannot chase one image after another but that one has to end all the images instantly, and not over a period of time. In order to get rid of these images, it is necessary to find out how these images get formed. Images are formed when the mind is not attentive, and images are based on conflict, and conflict is based on action. Thus, an image is formed when one of the two parties feels that the other has done something, which he or she should not have done; and, obviously, this image is based on self-interest. It is a fact of life that the isolation, which leads to loneliness, between the two parties in a relationship is based on a set of images, which are themselves based on actions, which have taken place over a period of time.

The entire set of images, which comes between the two parties in a relationship, gets shattered instantaneously, healing the distance between them only if it is possible for each to accept, totally, the basis of every religion. This has, over a period, been overlooked by people because it has been clouded beyond recognition by a mass of concepts and rituals. This basis of every religion is contained in the following words of the Bible: "Thy Will be done." The basis of the Islamic religion is also the same. The Hindu religion goes a step further and says: "God is both the speaker and the listener." This may seem confusing, but the meaning is clear: the apparent human entity who speaks and the other who listens would not be able to do either if they were both unconscious. Therefore, it is Consciousness (or the Source) that functions through two human instruments, and brings about talking through one and listening through the other. In other words, everything in the world is a happening according to God's Will or the Cosmic Law, and no individual entity is capable of doing anything. Therefore, no human being can be blamed for any happening. The total acceptance of this basic concept would instantaneously demolish all sets of images, and completely bridge the distance between the two parties in any relationship. This is the only way a relationship could be both Human and Divine.

CRITICISM I

Perhaps another significant cause of human misery, besides loneliness, is the fact that the ordinary man keeps judging the other person on the basis of his own concepts.

Most people in any society resort to criticising in order to interfere. Perhaps this gives them a certain amount of pleasure, a certain gratification, in shaping something or even someone. How can one judge another person unless one has inspected and judged oneself? It clearly shows a lack of understanding of relationships. Judging oneself brings about genuine humility, not the humility of which one is conscious. In fact, it needs supreme humility in order for the ultimate understanding to happen. Indeed, is not absolute humility the understanding itself?

However, the ordinary man's intellect mostly knows only how to argue, and demands the final word as victory. It does not know how to discuss, and therefore cannot learn anything from discussion, particularly concerning itself. Unfortunately, this conviction can be observed even in people who, otherwise, have quite a high standard of culture.

This inadequate utilisation of the mind becomes even more clearly defined when the topic is personal. Whereas the controlled mind will receive personal criticism with intellect, even eagerness, seeking to understand and benefit by any truth it may recognise in the criticism, the usual intellect will fight back at once, using any argument, however inadequate.

What is the process of understanding something? How does one understand one's child? One observes, one watches him at play; one studies him in his different moods. One does not project one's opinion on to him. One is alertly watchful, actively aware.

The understanding of relationships, so vital in daily living, can come about only when the mind is silently aware, observing without being critical, condemning, or justifying. Constantly criticising and inflicting one's own personality obviously sours a relationship and finally leads to a great amount of conflict.

CONFLICT I

Why, really, is there conflict between 'me' and the 'other'? "Because the 'other' is difficult," one might say. Yet, dealing with a difficult person cannot be avoided altogether. In such a situation, the man of understanding is fully aware that the 'other' – the difficult person – is not a happy person. He, therefore, will not treat the 'other' as an opponent or an adversary.

With this basic understanding, one would naturally meet this man not with a frown but a genuine smile of welcome. This may, in the beginning, confuse him, but it does not matter because there is nothing phoney in the smile since the basis of that smile is the understanding that the 'other' truly had no option in the situation, which is basically not anyone's doing, but a happening that has to happen according to God's Will or the Cosmic Law.

Then, what one would do is to begin the talk, not as a quarrel in which only one has to win and the other must lose, but as a problem for which both have to find a solution. In other words, the whole point is not to treat the 'other' as a difficult person.

The following situation gives a good example. We have a maid to help with the housework. One day, she requested leave on the following Sunday – a busy day for us – for urgent personal work. My wife agreed and made other arrangements. On Saturday, the maid, very regretfully, said that something had gone wrong and the arrangement had to be postponed to the following Sunday. Although the 'other arrangements' were much more difficult the next time, my wife agreed.

When our neighbour heard of the incident she was furious, and reprimanded my wife: "This is how you spoil the servants – you should have refused on principle." My wife's answer was: "What is the 'principle'? 'Might is right', or a harmonious relationship between two human beings?"

This is an extremely important factor if one wishes to live a life, inwardly and outwardly, without conflict, in peace and harmony. The basis of conflict is always the separation between 'me' and the 'other'. This separation, this division, is based entirely on doership: the 'other' is doing or saying something that 'I' don't like!

This separation between 'me' and the 'other' can disappear only if one is able to accept, totally, that everything is a happening according to God's Will or the Cosmic Law. And this basic fact of life should be self-evident. It is the experience of everyone that, having done whatever one wanted to do according to one's own free will, what actually happens has never been in one's control.

Why, then, blame anyone for anything that is, basically, a 'happening'? It is only this total conviction that bridges the apparent separation between 'me' and the 'other'. What such an acceptance brings about is a harmonious relationship between 'me' and the 'other' – whoever the 'other' is, a close relative or a total stranger. And this harmonious relationship obviously means the absence of all conflict.

REVALUATION OF VALUES

When thinking about relationships, love, conflict, and so on, one might ask oneself the following question: "Someone who has always been considered a friend says or does something, which hurts me deeply. How would I react?"

The usual two ways would be: either, considering oneself to be a 'good' person, always forgiving others for being weak, one suppresses the hurt and decides to be magnanimous and forgives him; or, one berates the 'friend' and, from then on, considers him a wicked man who has turned against one in spite of all that one may have done for him.

But there is a third way based on one's total acceptance that, as the Buddha said 2500 years ago, everything is a 'happening' according to the Cosmic Law and not the deed done by any individual. The one who has been able to accept this concept totally, therefore, accepts the hurt as something which had to happen according to the same Cosmic Law and one's destiny. The individual entity, the instrument through whom the happening has happened, is truly irrelevant.

Therefore, the question of one's blaming the friend simply does not arise. One does his best to ignore the happening and does not react to it. Perhaps, in the meantime, the friend has realised his mistake and wishes that he had not done what he thinks he has done. He may even apologise, and no further harm will have been done.

This leads to a revaluation of friendship and other values in general. Thousands of years of conditioning has given the ordinary man a sense of values that is selfish and lopsided. He feels happy and proud when he is able to give some gift to another or is able to do something for the 'other'. But is it not conceivable that a revaluation of values is absolutely necessary in order to transcend the flow of life and feel the deep peace of living in freedom?

For example, giving something to someone, helping anyone to obtain or do anything he wants, may be gratifying to the one who gives. In fact, however, it means gratifying the fictitious 'self' of the person who gives, and affirming the giver's power over the one who receives – actually to render him a disservice. Though, of course, the recipient will thank the giver for rendering the receiver the apparent disservice. The revaluation of values can also be seen in the fact that when a beggar renders another the service of accepting a rupee, the beggar thanks the giver for the opportunity of rendering that service. That is what the revaluation of values means. *In the revaluation of values, 'gratitude' would exist on both sides.* It means a true vision of a happening. One can render a service to somebody, and the only service one can render anybody, is to give the latter an opportunity of depriving himself of something, and thus of weakening the stranglehold of his fictitious self thereby.

Revaluation of values means accepting everything as a happening and not something done by someone for somebody else's benefit. Furthermore, it brings peace and harmony because one does not blame anyone for anything – neither oneself nor the 'other'. This must be applied to everything within the reach of the mind, down to all the apparent facts and circumstances of daily living. The revaluation of values enables one to live on the plane of Reality, with the total apperception that love and sacrifice are no longer two things, that everything is happening according to the Cosmic Law. *No one gives and no one receives – a happening has happened.*

PURSUIT OF PLEASURE 1

What does 'daily living' mean for most ordinary men and women? To be honest, what it means is interest in one's job, interest in one's progress, getting a better position, more prestige, more power. In other words, 'me' first and everyone else later. And, with that, there is often a feeling of guilt because one thinks it is wrong. But what is wrong about it?

Why bring in that factor at all? Because there are a few people who are not that self-centred and seem to prefer doing something for others. But, the fact of the matter is that the one who does something for others, does so because it gives him greater pleasure, greater satisfaction – the same thing, pursuit of pleasure, satisfaction. Why bring in an ideological concept? What one seeks, clearly, is pleasure, satisfaction, whether it is in sex, in freedom, or helping others, in becoming a great saint, or a powerful politician, or whatever. It is all the same process: pursuit of pleasure. Most human beings want, desire, search for, and crave for satisfaction. Why is one dissatisfied? Because, for example, one is married and that does not give him or her satisfaction; one goes to meetings and that means nothing; one looks at trees and nature, and feels nothing; and so, gradually, one is dissatisfied with everything one sees or has, or has felt. One wants more and more of what one does not have. Many ordinary men want and crave for position. Why? If one gives this matter a little thought, one cannot but come to the simple but bitter conclusion that one craves for a position which will be gratifying because, inwardly, one is just a shoddy little person, with all sorts of dogmas, belief in God, rituals and all that – a whirlpool of mischief and misery.

The pursuing or demanding of pleasure causes a tremendous amount of distortion. Not that pleasure is wrong. It is lovely to enjoy the sky, the moon, the stars, the clouds, the hills, and the shadows, but the distorting factor is the thinking mind wanting more and more all the time, with more variety.

It is most interesting to watch the process and pattern of the pleasure one is seeking. One finds that all one's judgements are based on likes and dislikes, which is, in fact, a habit one has cultivated through pleasure. When there is no pursuit of pleasure – something in the illusory future – there is genuine appreciation of what is present now. I look at that tree, the beauty of the leaves, the branches, and the curve of the tree. When I really look, whether it is at the tree, the rainbow, the fly, or a beautiful woman or a well-built man, in that look there may be satisfaction but not 'pleasure'. The pleasure only arises when involved thinking, in horizontal time, happens, giving rise to unnecessary sensuality, leading to further involvement.

Witnessing the process of pleasure is interesting because it makes the mind much more sensitive, and therefore, much more intelligent, much more objective. Now, this intelligence is operating: not 'my' intelligence, just intelligence. This intelligence has seen that the pursuit of pleasure inevitably breeds dullness and indifference. One looks at that tree, the beauty of the branch, the beauty of the curve of the tree, at a beautiful face, a well-proportioned body. When one really looks, totally, there is neither pleasure, nor judgement.

The pleasure only arises when thinking comes in: the beauty of the face, the walk, the dress. A second later, the thought comes in: *That was a beautiful woman*. And all the imagery, sex, intimations, and thrills begin. It is the thinking, which brings the rubbish with it.

Witnessing this, the mind has become extremely sensitive, disciplined, and now sees that the continuity of pleasure is created by thinking. *Why can't I just look at that tree, that woman, or that car? Why do thinking and judgement have to come into it?* The answer is simple: "I cannot prevent the thought from arising, but I do not have to get involved in it." It is the pursuit of pleasure – not the pleasure itself – leading first to seek more and more of the same thing, proceeding to a variety of items, and finally leading to a total indifference, which can cause severe depression, leading even to suicide.

A really basic question is: What is it that creates a fragmentary, neurotic mind, which breeds deception and illusion? If one gives this matter some deep thought, one has to come to the conclusion that the factor of distortion is 'thinking'. But, not thinking in the present moment – that is the 'working mind' – but the 'thinking mind' functioning in horizontal time that cultivates fear and promises pleasure. When the working mind functions rationally, objectively, sanely, thinking and judgement won't be distorting factors.

What one really seeks is the freedom from the thinking mind or involvement, which creates the pursuit of that pleasure, which means frustration. The thinking mind, demanding pleasure, pursues the experience and sustains the memory. Yet, watching the mind passively is, indeed, the discipline in which there is no suppression, and therefore, the mind becomes sensitive, disciplined. It sees that it is the thinking that has created the continuity of pleasure, and that such thinking has become a habit.

The answer is to enjoy the pleasure totally, completely, live with it, and be done with it. The mind is thus free from the known. This is what happens in the case of a man of understanding.

PROCESS OF THINKING I

It is also a fact of life that thinking has given most people a great deal of pleasure. Pleasure is entirely a guiding principle in life. The pleasure of any incident – any sensory pleasure – is recorded and thought over. So, thinking, as pleasure, plays a very significant part in daily living; thinking gives nourishment and vitality to an incident that has already become the past. It is not difficult to see that pleasure is always in the past; the imagined pleasure of tomorrow is still the recollection of the past, projected into the future.

The world has given so much importance to thinking and conceptualising. The ordinary man lives by thinking, he does things by thinking, he plans his life by thinking, his action is motivated by thinking. And thinking is worshipped, throughout the world, as the most important thing. But can thinking solve one's problems in daily living? Thinking has never solved any problems. Recent discoveries and other events have not been the result of human thinking, but inspirational thoughts and insights from the Source or Reality.

Obviously, one has to think – and go into the past – when one is doing something as a job: technologically, in the office, or in the kitchen. There is the rationality, the logic of thinking in action, in doing. But, the problem arises when horizontal thinking (in time) becomes irrational, when it sustains pleasure or fear.

It is so very important to make a clear distinction between thinking – thought being given – in the technological field, and conceptualising about what happens in life.

All books, all literature, everything is conceptualising, ending in concepts. And the ordinary man's relationship is based on conceptualising. One's wife is the image one has created by conceptualising, put together by all the things which go on between husband and wife – pleasure, sex, the irritations, the exclusions, and all the separative instincts that go on. Thinking – conceptualising and objectifying – is clearly the response of memory – memory as knowledge, as experience, as impressions – which has been accumulated, stored up in the brain cells.

It is necessary to understand the process of 'thinking'.

Thinking is the response of the accumulated memory – whether it is one's own, or the inherited, the communal experience and so on – and, thus, the response of the past, which may project itself into the future, going through the present, modifying it as the future. But it is still the past. Thus, thinking, based on the past, projects 'what-should-be' in the future – and so, there is conflict.

However, between thoughts there is a period of silence that is not related to the thinking process. One will observe that that period of silence, that interval, is not of time – it is the timeless – and along with the discovery and experiencing of that interval there is liberation from the conditioning of the mind.

It is only in that moment, when the mind is not giving continuity to the thinking process, that there is a stillness that is not induced, and there can be freedom from the conditioning of background.

In fact, most of one's problems are the result of 'thinking' because – unless it is in the laboratory or on the drawing board – 'thinking' is always self-perpetuating, self-centred, and conditioned.

One can only find a solution to a problem – individual or collective – when the process of thinking, which has its source in the 'me', in the background of tradition, of prejudice, and of conditioning, has come to an end. All thinking is based on the conceptual 'me', and the core of this 'me' is the sense of personal doership, chasing some object of desire all the time.

In order to live one's life without conflict in one's relationship with the 'other' – whoever the 'other' is – all that is necessary is to be constantly, deeply aware of how pernicious thinking can be. Then, it is possible to live in the 'what-is', without creating the all illusory 'what-should-be'. The mind that is quiet, and not distracted by its own conceptualising, can face the problem simply and directly and spontaneously arrive at the solution.

The Self is a problem that thinking can never resolve. It is, therefore, so very necessary to be aware of the mechanism of thinking, of the subtle and complicated movement of thinking. To be aware without condemnation or justification of the activities based on the 'me'-centre. Being totally aware of the process of 'thinking', which leads nowhere, is the only way for a state of intelligence, which is totally free of all conditioning, to arise.

The heart is not open when the mind considers each one a potential enemy. Once one has accepted that no one, including oneself, can be one's enemy then the heart is totally open to whatever is happening but the mind is silent. The heart is what one feels; the mind is what one thinks. The man of understanding does not care at all whether anybody considers him a man of understanding or not. He is not looking for fame or recognition.

Thinking that the 'other' is an enemy is one's mind living one's life. Feeling that nobody can possibly be an enemy is when the heart lives one's life. Now one's relationship with the 'other' is not only good for oneself but also good for the 'other'.

When there is no mind, what exists is the Impersonal Awareness or God, one's true nature.

Ultimate understanding can only be in the heart, never in the mind. Therefore, the man of understanding only functions from his heart. Whatever is happening is witnessed by the heart. The One has become all of us. Only if one does not forget it will there not be any trouble.

SPONTANEITY I

It is an everyday experience that when one's 'conscious' mind cannot provide an answer to a problem, the answer comes to us when we 'sleep on it', through the unconscious mind.

Therefore, there has to be the realisation of the limitations of the conscious mind, so that one does not force oneself to be unreasonably careful and only conscious of the 'me' as the doer of all actions. One must retain the liberty to have trust in that final authority which makes the grass grow and our limbs and organs work by themselves. Otherwise, anxiety and self-consciousness will destroy the sensitivity that is so necessary for decisions to be arrived at.

What actually happens in life is that the human being attaches undue importance to past conventions or conscious thinking, to communications by linear signs and mathematical symbols and not nearly enough to the intuitive feel, far more to the central spotlight vision and not enough to the perceptual, peripheral vision, far more to the analytical data and not enough to the 'gut-feeling'.

What is necessary is certainly not surrender to an impulse, but a rational recognition of a natural intelligence that can clearly be seen by the way we are able to breathe and move our limbs. As has been said, men are afraid to forget their own minds, fearing to fall through the void. The ordinary man is afraid to rely on the spontaneous functioning with which he is naturally endowed but which gets blocked through efforts to understand it in terms of conventional techniques.

Our physical actions – our bodily functions – happen without the need of thinking: "Do I have to eat? Do I have to go to the bathroom?" If all actions could happen equally spontaneously, without any thinking based on one's previous conditioning, life would be incredibly smooth and natural, without the burden of guilt and shame for one's actions, and the burden of hatred and malice towards the 'other'. The reason is simple: Life is *happening*; no one is *doing* anything.

This is what is seen in the way a man of understanding lives his life from day to day: an absence of the regularity and symmetry that is predictable. Instead, what is seen is something

Enigma?

apparently eccentric and disorderly, and yet uncommonly well-balanced, throbbing with a natural vitality.

To others, it seems that whatever the man of understanding does becomes successful, and they wrongly ascribe this to his powers. His success is actually due mostly to a sense of confidence, a lack of self-frustrating anxiety. He is usually an enigma to other people, his actions seem unpredictable precisely because they are natural and spontaneous.

It is important to realise that spontaneity and naturalness cannot be achieved. As the Zen poem puts it, "You cannot have it by taking thought, you cannot seek it by not taking thought." Understanding this fact is all that is required. Whether spontaneity happens or not would truly depend entirely on one's destiny according to God's Will or the Cosmic Law. One simply cannot forget this basic and ultimate fact of life.

The essential point is that in daily living, the total operation of the intellect is as natural as the formative behaviour of plants or birds. There has to be a certain spontaneity, which cannot be there if there is constant analysis and discipline. In other words, there is a beautiful, natural blending of discipline and spontaneity – discipline not being constrictive, and spontaneity not being wanton.

SELF-CONTROL THROUGH DISCIPLINE?

What is implied in discipline? Most people feel that they must, through some kind of discipline, subjugate or control the brute in them. The real point is: Should it be done through discipline or through an intelligent understanding of the Self itself?

The ordinary man might see someone whom he considers happy or even self-realised. He imitates him, and this imitation is called discipline. By practising a certain rule, a certain discipline, does he get freedom? Any form of compulsion denies freedom, inwardly and outwardly. Only virtue gives that freedom. Greed is confusion, anger is confusion, and bitterness is confusion.

The difficulty is that one has read so much and has

superficially followed so many disciplines because one has been told that if one practices these things over a number of years one shall have God at the end of it. But is God a mere marketable thing: "I give you this and you give me that?"

Discipline, conformity, and practice only give emphasis to self-consciousness as being something. The mind practices non-greed but it is not really non-greedy because it is not free from its own consciousness as being non-greedy. It has merely taken on a new look, which it calls non-greed.

To be clearly aware of this self-enclosing process is the beginning of intelligence. When one clearly sees this process of conflict, then one understands, from moment to moment, the ways of conflict. Once the intention is there, the inner sensitivity is in the picture all the time, so that this 'inner' will project that picture the moment one becomes quiet. And sensitivity can never come into being through compulsion.

The unknown needs freedom and not the pattern of the mind. What is essential is the tranquillity of mind. But it is so important to realise that when the mind is conscious that it is tranquil, it is no longer tranquil. The ordinary man is afraid to go wrong. Thus, fear is at the root of the desire to be disciplined, but the unknown cannot be caught in the net of discipline.

FEAR I

Then again, like the pursuit of pleasure, thinking gives rise to the appearance of fear: fear of the possibility of repeating what I did yesterday, fear of the recurrence of pain I had a week ago. Thinking sustains and nourishes the fear: fear of the present and future, fear of death, fear of the unknown, fear of not being loved. So, there is the rationality of thinking and the irrationality of thinking. There is the obvious rationality of thinking in technological matters – for example, in the office or in the kitchen. There is the rationality, the logic of thinking in action, in doing. But thinking becomes totally irrational when it sustains either pleasure or fear.

A study of the anatomy of fear would enable one to clearly

understand the phenomenon of fear itself. Both the interrelated manifestations of aggressiveness and fear have their base in desire. The need for the gratification of desire causes aggressiveness. Then, fear arises because of the possibility of not achieving it.

The physical aspects of the phenomenon of fear are simple enough: it is an allied aspect of self-preservation and is useful as the reflex that keeps one from being scorched or prepares one to face any imminent danger. This is totally different from the psychological fear or anxiety about not achieving something. This kind of fear soon becomes a habit that keeps infusing toxicity into the biological system, and, over a period of time, ruins the very mechanism of the psychosomatic apparatus that constitutes our body, adversely affecting the performance of the apparatus which, in turn, further increases the fear.

If one feels a particular relationship is beautiful, one does not want it to end. There is the idea that it might come to an end, and one is afraid of that. This is one part of the structure of fear. The other is: "I have known security, certainty, and tomorrow is uncertain; and I am afraid of that." Then, the problem arises: "How am I not to be afraid?"

The knowledge of yesterday, of many thousands of yesterdays, has given to the mind a certain sense of security – knowledge being experience, remembrance, and memories.

Knowledge is accumulation. If one had knowledge of tomorrow, one would not be afraid. One is afraid of what human beings have done to him or to another human being, and that knowledge is a scar on the mind.

The memory of that hurt is so deep that one even resists human relationships because of the fear of being hurt again. Knowledge brings fear of the future. Therefore, the question is: "How am I to be free of the scar of the past, and not project that knowledge into the future?"

If one lives in the past one is already dead. That feeling of living in the past is suffocating. One is frightened, frightened of tomorrow. In consequence, one is afraid of living and one is afraid of dying.

When one looks at the whole phenomenon of fear, its whole structure and its various forms, what is the root of fear? The whole process is a form of 'becoming' or 'being'. When the 'being' now is threatened then 'becoming' in the future is also threatened, and that creates fear. But is there really anything to 'become'? One can understand becoming healthier, or growing one's hair longer, but psychologically, what is there to become?

One has an image about oneself. And then, another person comes along and puts a pin in it, and that hurts. This knowledge has left a mark on the brain as memory, and this acts as a resistance, as a wall. So the question is: "Why do I have to have an image about myself at all – good, bad, noble, ignoble, ugly, or dull?" Thought has created an image because it wants security in that image. The image is built by thought and thought is seeking security.

So, can the mind *not* be hurt at all? Which means, not to have any kind of image? 'Thought' – whether it is an individual or a collective thought (culture, education, tradition, nationality, economic and social conditions) – has implied, in the mind, this sense of comparing an image with another image. And one must understand that as long as one has an image there will be the possibility of being hurt.

There is another, more significant, aspect of the whole issue of the psychological fear of being hurt. One may feel terribly hurt at what someone says, but may not react in the same way if, for instance, a machine were to say the same thing. If one is able to accept, totally, that whatever happens is a happening that had to happen according to God's Will or the Cosmic Law – through whichever body-mind organism – then the 'who' becomes irrelevant and redundant.

One would, then, not have the need to fear anyone as someone who could hurt him. In other words, if one is hurt psychologically, one is more concerned with the doership than with the hurt. If some machine were to tell someone something that was wanting in him, he would be inclined not to take offence and may even wonder if there could be some truth in it.

What is 'becoming'? Changing images? Changing one image for another image? Obviously so. One wants to become a kinder man, a more self-confident man, or whatever. But if one has no image at all, and one sees the reason for not having one logically, one also sees the truth – that images prevent relationship, whether it is the hurt image or the pleasant image.

If one has a pleasant image about another person, he considers him his friend, and if not, he regards him as an enemy. Why have any image at all? If one does apply oneself, and work at it, then one finds that there is a mind, there is a brain that can never be hurt, because there is nothing to be hurt. Who is it who feels the hurt? That is the question. The answer: it's only an image.

If one understands the whole nature of fear, then, as one observes, one is not only aware of the superficial, conscious fears, but is also able to penetrate deeply into the inner recesses of the mind. Then, fear ends and distortion ends too.

That means complete silence. Be completely silent and – out of that silence – use knowledge. This is spontaneity, absence of personal doership, and the total acceptance that everything is a happening according to God's Will or the Cosmic Law and not the doing by any separate entity.

Acceptance of the 'what-is' means the absence of fear.

SELF-IMAGE AND IMAGINATION I

One has what Freud called the narcissistic image. Narcissus, who saw the image of a beautiful man in the water, fell in love with it and, not being able to get to that image, pined away and died. The irony is that he already had that for which he was craving; he already was that for which he was pining.

The point is that when one produces this self-image in fantasy, it then becomes the thing longed for, and it creates the need to have *that*. But we are *that* already.

What is 'imagination' really, other than 'making an image', seeing the image of something that is not there? The fact of the matter is that there is no basic difference between the process of imagination and the process of perception. Indeed, the entire consciousness is actually created by a process, guided by information from the senses.

When one starts to imagine things which are not there, it could be called creative imagination. Then, there is another kind of imagination which comes from the past, from reflexes – the reflexive imagination – fantasy or fancy.

Reflexive imagination could be useful by imagining things and ways of doing things or solving problems. But it can also be dangerous, because this fantasy may slip over into apparent perception that can make one an entirely different person.

Therefore, imagination can be creative and it can also be destructive, because the fantasy realm can merge with reality and create a resistance to seeing that it is fantasy. The beautiful fantasies feel so good that they resist thoughts which say they are not right. This is how thought can enter into perception. And even when one does not think one is fantasising, it is still entering perception because perception is basically of the same nature as imagination. Knowing this will make one be more careful and alert.

KNOWING ONESELF I

The Greeks, the Hindus, and the Buddhists have said: "Know yourself." It is different from having a self-image and, thus, one of the most difficult things to do. In order to observe oneself, one must understand what is meant by 'observing'.

When one looks at a tree, there is not only physical distance between the tree and oneself, there is also a psychological distance. If one looks at a tree without a single image – without a single thought of like or dislike or whatever – then, for the first time, one sees the tree as it is and one sees the beauty of it, the vitality of it.

To observe oneself in this way – without the observer – is much more difficult. Therefore, one must find out who the observer is. What is the nature, the structure of the observer who is observing? Obviously, the observer is the past knowledge collected as conditioning, and, therefore, the discriminations and condemnations take place. Is it possible to watch oneself in action, in relationships, without any movement of the past?

When there is no observer, then there is only the observed. To observe the whole relationship – the whole series of actions – without condemning, justifying, naming, or labelling, means that the mind is no longer wasting energy on imagination or a self-image. It is then aware and has energy to deal with the situation that exists in that moment. If one is greedy, envious, or violent, it takes honesty to know, to understand, that one is greedy, envious, or violent. To pursue an ideal of non-greed, of non-violence, away from 'what-is', is, in fact, an escape which prevents one from discovering and acting directly upon what one is. To understand this obvious fact needs an extraordinary perception.

The understanding of what one is, without distortion, is the beginning of virtue – whatever one is, ugly or beautiful, wicked or mischievous. And virtue gives freedom. It is only in virtue that one can live, one can discover 'what-is'. But it must be clearly understood, again, that there is a basic difference between *being* virtuous and *becoming* virtuous.

Being virtuous comes through the understanding of

'what-is', whereas becoming virtuous – cultivation of virtue – means covering up 'what-is' with what one would like to be. The immoral man who is striving to become virtuous can never know virtue. To understand 'what-is' needs freedom from the fear of 'what-is'.

DESIRE

A matter of deep curiosity and some concern is: Does the man of understanding have desires? Desires that are based on the natural functions of the body-mind organism, obviously, cannot be avoided by anyone, for instance, hunger or thirst. Such basic desires existed even prior to any contact with some objects and must, therefore, continue to exist in the case of a man of understanding, as with others.

Other than desires based in the natural functions, all other desires are the basic cause of bondage. Daily living seems to have a pattern: being dissatisfied with the one particular object of desire, one finds a substitute for it. One is everlastingly moving from one object of desire to another, which is considered to be higher, nobler, or more refined. And in this pursuit of desire there is endless conflict.

For instance, one desires some transformation because there is pain, discomfort, conflict and one wants something better, something nobler, more idealistic. Being in a state of conflict, one wants to achieve a state in which there is no conflict.

It is a common saying that resistance to conflict is necessary in order to overcome the conflict and, for that, one needs time to practise non-violence, non-envy, and peace. But the fact of the matter is that the very resistance to conflict is, itself, a form of conflict. It is therefore necessary to see the falsity of the process of depending on time in order to overcome conflict.

What is the process of desire? There is perception, sensation, and contact, and the mind becomes the mechanised instrument of this process, the centre of which is the 'me'. When one is aware of this whole structure of desire, one sees how the mind has become a dead centre, a mechanical process of memory. Being bored with a particular sensation, one seeks a new sensation – maybe the 'realisation of God' – but it is still a sensation. In other words, the mind has become a stagnant pool of the past.

The problem is, therefore, whether the mind can ever be free from desire, from sensation. The mind's approach has always been through memory and recognition, and is, therefore, incapable of experiencing anything new.

The point to remember in daily living is that no positive action, like suppressing desire, could ever achieve any success in destroying desire. On the contrary, any positive action will only strengthen desire. The only way to destroy desire is to witness, passively, the arising of desire each time it happens. Such passive witnessing without involvement cuts off the desire and prevents it from extending itself horizontally, through its pursuit.

Beyond the physical needs, any form of desire – including truth or virtue – becomes a psychological process, through which the mind strengthens the 'me', the centre of desire. The ordinary man realises that process but, in his misunderstanding, considers himself in control of a change for the better. At this point, the urge for self-improvement often comes in, yet another desire.

It is only when one sees this process in its entirety and accepts it without any kind of judgement, without a sense of temptation and wanting, without resistance, that the mind becomes capable of receiving Reality – a state in which creativeness can happen without invitation, without memory.

SELF-IMPROVEMENT 1

Quite often, the ordinary man feels a strong desire to improve. Self-improvement is obviously based on time. One seems to be moving from the past towards the future, but that experience does not make sense because the future really does not exist. It is not spread out before one. All one has is the present moment, the Now.

Even this physical fact must start from the present. Physics can establish a fact of the order of succession. But that order cannot be so nicely established psychologically. One can hardly remember very much of what happened in the past, and it has been proved that it is mostly invented anyway. And the future is an expectation, which is seldom realised.

When one says: "I expect to be successful in changing myself for the better in the future," one is counting on time and some order of necessity in that succession. Actually, it is all contingent – that is a fact. One may intend to arrive there but one may actually arrive somewhere else altogether.

If one is going on a trip from one point to another, according to a particular route on the map, this will probably happen. But, if one says, "I am going to go through a series of steps in self-improvement," in most cases it may not happen. In fact, all these psychological steps are rainbows that one is chasing.

Yet, for life to be more meaningful, more fulfilling, one feels there must be change in oneself – the more sensitive, the more alert and intelligent one is, the more intensely one is aware that there must be a deep, abiding, living change. This can only relate to one's attitude towards life. One is aware from personal experience that one has absolutely no control over the *flow* of life and the only control one may have is over one's *attitude* to life.

One thinks one cannot possibly change; one feels forced to accept things as they are and becomes depressed, dispirited, uncertain, and confused. But down the ages, the men and women of understanding have averred, and themselves proved, that it is possible for one to change radically. Yet, that change entirely depends on God's Will, the Cosmic Law. Even the personality of the man of understanding has positive and negative aspects. The man of understanding accepts this duality, and has humility, which leads to tolerance of the 'other's' negative aspects.

For a change in one's attitude towards life it is necessary to be aware of 'what-is' in the moment, throughout the day, without even wanting to correct anything in the future – just being aware of it. So, during the day, if one is deeply aware of the warp of one's thoughts, one's motives, the hypocrisy, the double-talk – doing one thing, saying another, thinking a third – the mask one puts on, without blaming oneself or wanting to change oneself, then, when one goes to sleep, the process has totally come to an end, no memory is recorded in the mind, things have been seen exactly as they are, and not the interpretation or the desire to change them.

In other words, the whole nervous system has become totally quiet, and the sleep has become totally different. Things can be seen exactly as they are, not in one's interpretation of them or the desire to change them in the course of time. This means peace and harmony in daily living.

ASPECTS OF TIME I

Time has various aspects in daily living. Depending on the subject, one can differentiate between physical and mental time on the one hand and chronological and psychological time on the other.

First, there is physical and mental time. There is only one way to explain the difference between the two: sensory experiences, feelings or decisions, for example, occur in sequence. What separates one experience from the next one? It is called 'time', noting the extent to which the memory of a past experience has faded. So the fading of the memory is one way of estimating how long ago that experience was.

When one is young and inexperienced everything is new and catches the attention – one is laying down memories at a furious rate. As one gets older and more worldly-wise – perhaps 'jaded' – most experiences are so familiar they are liable to pass by without being recorded as faithfully as in the past. It will then seem that not much has happened since a particular event. In other words, not much time has elapsed, a conclusion contradicted by the calendar.

It is significant to note that although we use the word 'time' to describe the separation between our mental experiences, it is different when used in the description of what is going on in the physical world. For one thing, mental states occur in time but not in space. One does not ask how much space a big decision like getting married takes up, compared to a small decision. And yet, one knows how indissoluble the link between physical time and physical space is.

What this means is that all physical time exists at the instant of mental time called 'Now'. The 'Now' of mental time is correlated to a particular instant of physical time. In other words, although all physical time exists now, Consciousness singles out one particular instant as having special significance for the 'Now' of mental time.

That conscious focus then appears to move steadily along the time axis in the direction labelled 'future'. But it is important to understand that this so-called movement is not out there in the physical world itself – it is a feature only of one's conscious experience of that physical world. The 'flow' is only in the mental time.

Then there is chronological time, as yesterday, today, and tomorrow, and psychological time, for example, as part of the fear: "I am afraid of tomorrow and I don't know how to meet that fear of tomorrow." The time that one is really concerned with in daily living is not the chronological time, which is taken care of by daily routine and habit.

It is the 'psychological' time that creates problems for the human being. The ordinary man's mind, his activities, and his very being are founded on psychological time. Thinking horizontally, getting mentally involved, is based on time. Time is memory. One seems to spend most of the time thinking over what has happened in the past and what one wants in the future. The present is merely the passing of knowledge of the past to the future. The memory of yesterday's experience in response to the present is creating the future.

It is everyone's experience that when one is in deep joy, listening to his favourite music, or whatever, in that moment there is no time, only the present moment. The mind, which is the experiencer, comes into the picture later and wants to prolong the experience. It should, therefore, be obvious that efforts to discipline the mind in time duration cannot possibly reveal that, which is timeless.

When one no longer depends on time as a means of transforming 'what-is' – because one sees the falsity of the process – only then is one confronted with 'what-is'. It is necessary to understand the 'what-is' instead of pursuing an illusory 'what-should-be'. Then, the mind becomes quiet and, in that passive but alert state of mind, understanding can happen. So long as the mind is in conflict, blaming, resisting, condemning, there cannot be understanding.

When the mind is still, tranquil, not seeking any answer or solution – neither resisting nor avoiding – only then can there be regeneration. *Regeneration can only be now, not tomorrow.* The mind in that state is capable of receiving what is true. It is truth that liberates, not the effort to be free.

FREE WILL AND EFFORT

Is it not a plain, simple fact that this exercise of supposed choice and action, which is free will, is what actually causes 'bondage' and the ensuing conflict and suffering due to a supposed need to 'do' something? The question of individual choice and personal effort in daily living has caused a certain amount of difficulty.

Difficulty arises because most men of understanding, or Masters, seem to have taught predetermination in theory and free will in practice. Jesus Christ affirmed that without God's Will, not even a sparrow will fall and that the very hairs on one's head are numbered. The Quran affirmed that all knowledge and power is with God and that "He leads aright whom He will and leads astray whom He will." And yet, both oblige men to right effort and condemn sin.

There is really a simple explanation for this apparent contradiction. The human being seems to make the effort, but the actual fact is that it is the primal energy that functions through every human body and brings out that effort, which the body is to produce according to its programming (genes plus conditioning). Also, once the effort has happened, what actually happens as a result or consequence has never been in anyone's control.

The man of understanding is indifferent to the way the sense organs react to the sense objects. He does not hanker after more pleasure, nor does he refuse whatever comes his way. Wanting something positively or not wanting something negatively are both aspects of free will and personal doership. In the case of the man of understanding, the absence of free will includes the absence of identification as a separate entity because it is the very core of identification.

The understanding of the fact that all interrelated opposites – likes and dislikes – are the cause of conceptual bondage is itself the liberation from the concept of bondage. The man of understanding does not get involved in daily life and living but merely witnesses it as a show.

In other words, the man of understanding does precisely what the ordinary man does but knows he has no choice, and does whatever he has to do *as if* he has it. The man of understanding does whatever he thinks he should do, but is totally aware that what actually happens depends not on what he wanted but strictly on God's Will or the Cosmic Law.

The man of understanding, while functioning in daily life as a separate entity, is fully aware that he is a character in the dreamed universe, and does not remain outside the dream as a separate observer of the dream. The result of any effort rests only on God's Will or the Cosmic Law. What is the value, then, of free will and 'personal' effort and the respective activity?

This vicious circle will only be broken by the clear realisation that the results of one's efforts have never been in one's control and that they depend, entirely, on one's destiny according to God's Will or the Cosmic Law. And this is, actually, everyone's experience: the same amount of effort sometimes brings success and sometimes does not. Realisation of this fact creates a sense of freedom from anxiety, which, in turn, releases an extraordinary amount of energy, which cannot but improve one's day-to-day performance beyond recognition. It is so much easier to float with the current than to swim against it.

ACTIVITY I

The basis of one's activity in daily living is reward in the future or fear of punishment. There is an idea of virtue, an ideal or a goal. 'Relationship', collective or individual, means action towards the ideal, towards achievement. Activity, in other words is, in fact, based on bridging the gap between 'what-is' and the illusory 'what-should-be'.

The ordinary man thinks: "I am not generous, but I want to be generous." But is any corrective action really necessary? If one truly realises the fact, not merely verbally or artificially, that one is not as generous or loving as another person, then, in that very seeing of 'what-is', is there not a total acceptance of generosity or love? Such spontaneous action is timeless, into which the calculating, dividing, and isolating process does not enter.

Such action can happen only when one truly realises, from one's own experience, that there really is no individually-done action, that all apparent action is, indeed, a happening according to God's Will or the Cosmic Law. Take for example the news about a railway accident in which everyone in the coach is either dead or injured, except one man who escapes without a scratch.

"All the world's a stage, and all the men and women merely players." Ramana Maharshi, a man of understanding who lived in Southern India in the first half of the twentieth century, said: "All the actions that the body is to perform are already decided upon at the time it comes into existence. The only freedom you have is whether or not to identify yourself with the body."

In other words, Ramana Maharshi tells us that a man's role as an actor is cast when he is born on to the stage of manifestation, and he has to play out his part as it is written by the Source. If he chooses to remember that he is only an instrument, through which the Source functions, and plays the part that he is to play, his 'acting' will be so natural that the spectators will be deeply moved and he will be acclaimed as a great actor.

It has been the experience of many genuine seekers that their work, whatever it is, has improved enormously since they were able to accept, totally, that everything is a happening according to the Cosmic Law and not the doing by any individual doer –

be it as an actor, lawyer, banker, or teacher.

Those who observe a man of understanding find that he says the same thing over and over again but each time it is totally natural and impeccably expressed.

One realises that all activities, based on identification with the body, with a particular group, with a particular desire, the glorification of an ideal, the pursuit of virtue, are essentially self-centred activities.

Religions, through promises, through fear of hell, through every form of condemnation, have tried to dissuade man from self-centred activity. These having failed, political organisations have taken over; every form of legislation has been used and enforced against any form of resistance. Yet, the ordinary man goes on with his self-centred activity, which seems to be the only kind of action he knows.

All such activity must come to an end voluntarily through understanding – not self-imposed, not influenced, not guided. This can happen only if one is able to accept, totally, the concept enunciated by the Buddha 2500 years ago: "Events happen, deeds are done, but there is no individual doer thereof." In other words, everything is a happening according to God's Will or the Cosmic Law. How it affects anyone depends, again, on the Cosmic Law or on one's destiny. Then, there is no question of any pride or guilt of any action that happens.

WORK

It is an astonishing fact that in spite of the universal experience that the result of one's efforts and activities is not in one's control – sometimes one gets what one expects, sometimes one does not get what one expects, and sometimes one gets what one never expected, for better or worse – the modern man works for results, especially success.

Modern man has somehow persuaded himself that he has no right to work unless he is paid for it. Full payment for work of any kind, for service of any kind, has acquired a character that is almost sacramental – not the work but the remuneration now has that character. This principle demands as much as can be extorted and gives as little as possible in return.

The Bhagavad Gita tells us:

1. "You must perform every action sacramentally, and be free from all attachment to results."
2. "You have the right to work. You have no right to the fruits of work."
3. "They who work selfishly for results are miserable."

The principle in the Bhagavad Gita makes it possible for the human being to be happy, because it means a daily living worthy of a self-respecting human being. In that way, man is free to develop spiritually. In the other, there is only misery and degradation. One has only to look around oneself for the proof.

There is, however, another view. Men and women should not be remunerated according to the status and degree of responsibility of the work they are able to do. The remuneration they receive should be for their living and not for their work. This would eliminate competition and rivalry among peers at the workplace.

This concept may seem strange to a modern man. However, it is a fact that this concept is normal and older than many of the scriptures – as old, indeed, as human civilisation. As recently as the end of the nineteenth century, not only were men in exalted and responsible positions so remunerated, performing their work as a service, but this was also the case for men and women in ordinary domestic employment. In those cases, as the basis of the contract, their lives were protected, they were cared for, received housing, food, clothing, and money for their personal needs. So it has been in all walks of life throughout history. This is clearly different from that which demands as much as can be extorted and gives as little as possible in return.

Yet, in that way, 'happiness' is possible and, consequently, also a life that is worthy of a self-respecting human being. In that way, man is free to develop spiritually. In the other way, there is only misery and degradation, based on selfishness and greed, as can be found today.

SUCCESS AND FAILURE I

Success and failure in life is entirely a matter of destiny; and this is why it is often seen that brilliant people are not really successful in life, while there are people of mediocre ability who are successful.

When this fact is not kept in mind, one finds the usual explanation and recrimination about success and failure – for instance, of a cricketing side. The side is expected to win but loses the match. The explanation promptly comes: "We batted badly, we bowled badly, and we fielded badly." This explanation is merely the description of the mechanics of the failure. This does not say 'why' they played badly. The answer really is obvious: they played badly because according to their destiny, God's Will, and the Cosmic Law, they were not supposed to win.

Some years ago, there was a lovely little book written by the president of a successful hire-purchase company. It was a remarkably successful book, mainly because of the transparent honesty with which it was written. The author confessed that his decisions were not always good decisions; many of them turned out to be bad, but he always admitted that the decisions were wrong, and took the necessary action to correct the mistakes as quickly as possible. His point was that several presidents of other companies were also found to have taken wrong decisions, but many, because of their egos, refused to accept they were wrong and persisted with them. In other words, according to the author, to err is human and honesty in recognising and accepting the mistake is evidence of successful leadership.

Then there is this instance – a true happening – in my own experience. When I was in charge of a particular region during my banking career, I came across a case of two friends running a flourishing concern. One was the owner of the concern and the other was his chief manager. Both were friends over a long period, ever since their school days. After the schooling, both started their own business. The manager was a brilliant student and was expected to do well, but, one after another, three of his efforts failed; whereas the owner, a middle-order student, was very successful from the beginning. The result was that they met one day and agreed upon the new arrangement, and the business had gone on from success to success thereafter, everything according to destiny, God's Will, and the Cosmic Law.

ORDER

It is important to understand that by 'order' I do not mean what many people consider it to be. One sees people who are supposed to be orderly, who have a certain rigidity, but no pliability. They are not quick, and have become rather hard and self-centred because they are following a certain pattern which they consider to be order, and soon that becomes a neurotic state.

Order does not mean habit. Habit makes human beings orderly only in the mechanical sense. Being aware of the disorder, the confusion all around, how is one to bring about order in oneself without any conflict and without its becoming merely habitual?

Surely, one must have physical order. A well-disciplined,

sensitive, alert body that reacts to the mind. Then there must be order in the whole totality of the mind, of the brain. The mind is the capacity to understand, the ability to observe logically, sanely, to function totally – all round, not fragmentally – not to be caught in contradictory desires, purposes, and intentions.

What is order then? There is the order of the older generation, which is really total disorder, as one observes its activities throughout the world – in business, in religion, in the economic field, amongst nations, and everywhere else. In reaction to that, there is the permissive society, the younger generation who do quite the opposite, which is also disorder. A reaction can only be disorder.

Can order be brought about through discipline, through conformity, imitation, and control? Or, is there really an order that has nothing to do with control, with discipline as we know it, with conformity, adjustment, and so on?

Now, what is implied in control? "I am angry, and I must control my anger." And where there is control there is conflict, which distorts the mind. Only a healthy mind can function without any friction. Such a mind is a sane, clear mind. But in control there is conflict and contradiction. So control is not order. This is important. Control implies suppression, conformity, adjustment, and the division between the observer and the observed.

The old culture has said that there must be discipline throughout life. The word 'discipline' means to learn. It does not mean drilling, conforming, suppressing. And the mind itself resists being drilled. The question, therefore, is how is order to come about without discipline in the accepted sense of the word?

One has to have order, something living and beautiful, not a mechanical thing – the order of the universe, the order that exists in mathematics, the order that exists in nature, in relationships between various animals, an order that human beings have totally denied. Within himself, the ordinary man is in disorder, which means that he is fragmentary, contradictory, and frightened.

When we see something really dangerous, a wild animal, or a man with a gun, we avoid it instantly. There is no arguing, no hesitation, no tempering – there is immediate, spontaneous action. In quite the same way when the danger of disorder is seen, there is instant, spontaneous action; and this action is the total denial of the whole culture which has brought about disorder.

What has brought about disorder is the sense of personal docrship, personal responsibility. And the fact of the matter is that truly, as the Buddha has declared, all there is at any time is a happening, which has happened through some body-mind organism, according to God's Will or the Cosmic Law. No one is to blame – neither oneself nor the 'other'. All that one can do consciously in any given situation is precisely what one thinks one should do. The results, of course, have never been in one's control.

I, personally, only know what disorder is; I am completely familiar with it, the whole culture of disorder in present society. But I do not really know what order is! One can imagine what order is, one can conceptualise about it, but speculation is not order. The mind knows what disorder is, how it has come into being through culture and the conditioning of that culture.

It is important to really know that state of mind of 'not knowing'. The state of 'not knowing' is not waiting to be told, not expecting an answer. It is very much alive, active. It knows what disorder is, and, therefore, rejects it totally, and, thus, it is totally free. It has denied disorder.

Because it is free of all concepts about order, it has already found order. Now the mind is capable of learning. When the mind is totally free – non-fragmented, whole, then it is in a state of order. Nobody, no teacher, no philosopher, no Master can teach what order is. Is one aware of all the movements and all the reactions that are going on within oneself during the day?

If one is aware during the day, watching, attentive to how much one eats, what one says, what one thinks, of one's motives, one would be aware of the jealousy, envy, greed, and violence. This, in consequence, would mean that one has brought order, not according to any plan, but just order. One has been aware of what has been happening. One has lived a disordered life of not being aware. When one has become aware of everything that has happened, there is order.

One is surely aware of one's life, or daily life, family life, and relationships with each other. And, in this life, one is aware of the daily routine, the monotony, the boredom, of the nagging, quarrels, the violence, which is the result of a culture that is in total disorder. And out of that disorder one cannot pick and choose what one thinks is order.

One has to observe oneself with great honesty, without any sense of hypocrisy or double talk – and then put aside that disorder so as to find out what order is. Putting aside disorder is not really difficult if one does not dramatise it, and make much of it.

Is it not a fact that in all these hundreds of years, humanity has not been able to find a solution to the outer chaos, confusion, brutality, violence, and other horrors? Therefore, one turns to the inner self and hopes to find a solution there. Then, not being able to find a solution to the inner chaos there, the inner brutality, violence, and all the rest of it, one moves away from both and seeks, out of desperation, some solution to the outer and the inner chaos, in a third, other dimension.

This, then, is the real, actual situation. Then, could it possibly be that the solution could lie in seeing the whole of this existence as one unitary interconnected movement, and not as a fragmented problem? Could it be that the solution is really a simple one because the cause of the confusion – both the inward and the outward, leading to the third beyond both – is itself a simple one?

This is, indeed, the fact of the matter. The entire confusion is based on the division between 'me' and the 'other', and the hatred between the two.

Man has believed that he, as a separate entity from the 'other', does whatever he wishes to do in any situation, and so does the 'other' – in a subject-object relationship. What each one does in any situation is often in conflict with what the 'other' wants, and this leads to hatred: hatred for oneself for hurting the 'other' and hatred for the 'other' for what he has done to oneself. And it is this load of hatred, which the ordinary man carries all the time, which is the cause of the confusion, both inner and outer, both individual and collective.

If this position is accepted, the solution becomes extraordinarily simple. It is everyone's personal experience that whatever one does in any situation is of one's own free will. Indeed, free will, for every individual human being, is the basis of the mechanism of daily living. Daily living cannot happen in the absence of free will for every human being. But it is also everyone's experience that once one has exercised one's free will and done whatever one wanted to do, it has always been God's Will about everything that has happened afterwards. Therefore, it is stupid to blame anyone for any happening, either oneself or the 'other'.

This is precisely the gist and significance of the Buddha's words: "Events happen, deeds are done, but there is no individual doer thereof."

GOOD AND EVIL I

One has watched, all over the world, the acceptance of killing in war, which is, surely, organised murder. Also, 'killing' people with words, with a gesture, a look of contempt, has also been decried by religious people. But in spite of it all, killing, violence, brutality, aggressiveness, and arrogance have been going on – all ultimately leading, in action or in thought, to hurting, to brutalising others. When one looks at all this, one wonders if there is such a thing as evil in itself, totally devoid of the good; and what the distance between evil and good is. Is evil the lessening of good, slowly ending in evil? Or good the lessening of evil, gradually becoming good? Are they two ends of the same stick or are they two wholly separate things. What is evil and what is good? The Christian world, during the days of the Inquisition, used to burn people for heresy, considering that was good. The communists do it their own way: for the good of the community, for the good of society, for the economic well-being of everyone.

Do good and evil exist absolutely, or are they simply the result of a conditioned point of view? Is there an absolute goodness and an absolute evil? The fact of the matter is that good and evil are the interconnected opposites, or counterparts, of one species of the basic duality that is the essence of manifestation and its functioning called life – duality of every conceivable type, beginning with male and female, beautiful and ugly, black and white, short and long, health and disease. One cannot get away from this basic fact: one says something is beautiful only because one has already decided that something else is ugly. In other words, where society is concerned, there cannot be good without evil, but the perspective is entirely different when the individual considers the issue from his individualist point of view: goodness could be considered as total order, especially inwardly – order in the mind, order in one's heart, order in one's physical activities. The harmony between the three could be considered 'goodness'. And, as most human beings live in disorder, they contribute to every form of mischief, which ultimately leads to distraction, to violence and brutality, to various injuries, both physical and psychic. It is clear, therefore, that where society is concerned, evil and good cannot exist separately but only as the interconnected opposites.

Where the individual is concerned, however, the perspective is totally different. 'Good' is that which brings about peace and harmony; 'evil' is that which prevents peace and harmony from happening. Peace of mind can happen only when there is total order in the body-mind organism, when there is total harmony in the relationship with the 'other'. The very basis of daily living is the relationship with the 'others', from morning till night – the 'other' may be a close relative, or someone connected with one's occupation, or even a total stranger. Unless the relationship with the 'other' is totally harmonious, there cannot be peace of mind. And it is a matter of practical experience that one's peace of mind is totally dependent on one's sense of personal doership. It is a matter of personal experience that peace of mind can never exist where there is a feeling of hatred. What the sense of personal doership creates is hatred: hatred for oneself for hurting others with one's deeds, and hatred for others for hurting one with their deeds.

It is the Buddha who has provided us with the solution for the problem of hatred: "Events happen, deeds are done, but there is no individual doer thereof." This clearly means that everything in life is a happening according to God's Will or the Cosmic Law and, therefore, no one can be blamed for any happening – neither oneself, nor the 'other'. The total acceptance of this concept means the total absence of any hatred, either for oneself or for the 'other'. And, the absence of hatred means the presence of a harmonious relationship with others and peace of mind for oneself. And, truly, this could be considered as absolute goodness in the individual entity.

MEDITATION 1

Modern man faces a problem: too much daily routine and not enough time for leisure. Meditation has become a luxury. The physical and mental benefits of meditation are recognised, but what is not recognised is: What is true meditation?

Surely it cannot mean locking oneself in a room, sitting down in front of a picture of one's guru, repeatedly reminding oneself that the back must be straight. This is not meditation. What is generally understood by the word 'meditation' is practising a system, a method, in order to achieve enlightenment – or bliss – or to have a quiet mind, or to achieve a state of tranquillity, or something like that.

But repeating something over and over again makes the mind

dull and mechanical. It implies suppression of one's own movement and understanding, and also means conformity that leads to endless conflict. The mind likes to conform to a system because it is easier to live that way.

Now, what is meditation? Is it, as has often been suggested, control of thinking? And if it is, who is the controller? Obviously, this could only be the thinker himself. Control implies imitation, conformity, acceptance of a pattern as authority according to that pattern, which is the existing society and culture. According to that pattern, one tries to live, suppressing all one's own feelings and ideas, trying to conform. In that conforming there is conflict. So, obviously, concentration, which is so often advocated in meditation, is totally incorrect.

Meditation, which means 'sitting thinking' or 'sitting thinking of not thinking', necessarily, requires a 'me'-entity doing the meditation. Meditation done with determination over a certain period will almost certainly produce some 'results', some kinds of experiences, which would encourage the meditator to do more.

The danger is that instead of the vital purpose of the demolition of the doership of the 'me'-entity, the 'progress' might actually strengthen the doership of the ego-entity and produce more and more expectation.

The root meaning of the word 'meditation' is to measure.

The whole Western world and its culture are based on the idea of measurement, but in the East they have said, "Measurement is illusion. Therefore one must find the immeasurable." So, the two drifted apart culturally, socially, intellectually, and religiously.

Events, technology, and the associated things that have been happening in the world have been producing great changes outwardly. Yet, inwardly, most people remain as they are. Any revolutionary change can take place only at the very centre of one's being, and requires an abundance of energy. And the release of that total energy is meditation. It is the discovery of that energy, which has no friction and is thus free and immeasurable.

Meditation is self-knowledge, and without self-knowledge there is no meditation. The basis of meditation is being aware of one's responses all the time, being truly aware. The one who is fully aware is meditating. Meditation, more accurately, is happening. The mind is really still. This stillness is not the weary dullness brought about through repetition, through regimentation, and all the rest of it.

If one really wants to know oneself, one will have to search out one's mind and heart to know their full content. One will have to follow, without condemnation or justification, every movement of thought and feeling as it arises. This will bring about that tranquillity which is not compelled, not regimented. It is very much like the pool that becomes quiet and peaceful any evening when there is no wind. Only when the mind is still, can that which is immeasurable come into being.

It is only when there is complete understanding of oneself, that there is the ending of conflict. And this is meditation. The absence of conflict means the happening of meditation throughout daily life without any meditator. And such meditation means peace and harmony in daily living.

Whenever I am asked whether one should meditate, or do some other spiritual practice, my usual answer is: "Yes, meditate if you like to meditate, but I wouldn't force myself to do so." My basic concept is that all 'doing' is not done by any individual entity, but that the doing happens because of the primal energy functioning through a particular body-mind organism, producing whatever is meant to be produced according to the Cosmic Law.

What actually happens in life is that, in any given situation, the separate entity does whatever he wishes to do according to his free will. But, apart from the fact that this 'free will' is entirely dependent on his genes and his conditioning – two factors, over which he had absolutely no control – what actually happens, may be quite different from his decision. Whether the decision turns into action, and whether the action results in the anticipated goal, depends entirely on God's Will, the Cosmic Law, and the destiny of the entity concerned.

In my own case, I did start the practice of meditation, and the practice of repeating a mantra, in the early stages of the seeking. At some point of time, because of the prevailing circumstances, 'doing' the practice stopped and, after a while, the meditation and the mantra repeating happened, not at specific times but at odd times.

These days, I wake up at around 5 am and, after morning ablutions, find myself relaxing in my usual rocking chair. The rocking ceases at some time, of which I am not really aware, and the meditation begins: sitting quietly, watching the breathing getting shallower and shallower, and then, suddenly finding that the meditation has ended after about forty to fifty minutes. Thereafter, the daily routine begins and ends in the evening. There never is a sense of 'doing' anything.

True progress in meditation can come about only when there is no ego-doer of the meditation, expecting a certain result as quickly as possible. True meditation is that which happens when there is no meditator evaluating the result of the meditation. This true meditation brings about freedom, clarity, and integration. Peace of mind in daily living.

Indeed, the understanding of the process of thinking is meditation. It is only when the mind is not giving continuity to the thinking process, when it is still with a stillness that is totally spontaneous and not induced, that there can be freedom from conditioning.

Meditation is the seeing of 'what-is' – seeing the measure and going beyond the measure. When the brain, the mind and the body are really quiet and harmonious, then one is able to live a totally different kind of life – accepting whatever happens as a happening according to the Cosmic Law, without blaming anyone for anything. This means a harmonious relationship with the 'other' and peace of mind within oneself.

DISPASSION I

In daily living, what does being 'dispassionate' mean? Dispassion does not mean disinterest in life. But, once dispassion arises, the individual concerned begins to question the validity of a happiness based on material objects that do not have any kind of consistency or permanency.

Experience tells everyone that objects that were considered to bring happiness soon fail to do so, and even bring unhappiness. Then, the individual's mind turns inward towards its true nature. Self-investigation begins, which eventually leads to the inexorable conclusion that everything is a happening according to God's Will or the Cosmic Law, and not the 'doing' of any individual entity. This means freedom from guilt, shame, and hatred towards the 'other'.

True dispassion cannot be brought about by austerity or by conscious good deeds or by pilgrimages. The earliest stirrings of dispassion can arise only through what might be called Divine Grace – what had to happen according to the Cosmic Law.

The early stirrings might arise suddenly and spontaneously, or there might be an apparent cause like a sudden serious difficulty or problem in life or a sudden bereavement in the family.

When dispassion persists and matures, it gradually transforms itself into the realisation that the true happiness a human being seeks lies not in the material pleasures that the flow of life might bring (because they cannot be separated from the pains which might follow), but in *one's attitude to the flow of life*. This happiness is nothing but peace of mind; this depends not on success or failure in life, but on the renunciation of the sense of personal doership that leads to guilt and shame for some of our own actions, and hatred towards the 'others' for their actions which might have hurt us. It is this load of hatred – both for oneself for one's own actions and for the 'others' for their actions – which comes between us and self-realisation. Dispassion leads to the total acceptance of personal non-doership, of the totality of functioning proceeding to unfold the play of the Grand Design.

SPIRITUAL SEEKING I

The most important fact in life is that any kind of seeking is not started by the seeker, but is a happening according to one's destiny, God's Will, or the Cosmic Law. Indeed, every body-mind organism is naturally programmed for a particular kind of life.

It is particularly important for the spiritual seeker to understand this fact: he did not start the spiritual seeking but it started on its own, as God's Will. Otherwise, the 'seeker', pursuing the seeking as his free will, is likely to be frustrated. The progress in the spiritual seeking must obviously depend also on God's Will or the destiny of the seeker.

If this fact is firmly kept in mind, then the seeker will not be under stress and, thus, be more open and receptive to suggestions from Consciousness, from 'outside'. Any action, based on free will, can only be an obstruction. The best progress can happen only when one goes with the flow of life, and all action becomes spontaneous.

Depending on the destiny of a particular spiritual seeker, awakening may occur. In that context, the statement of a Zen Master: "Awakening is sudden, deliverance may be gradual," has caused a certain amount of confusion. The meaning, however, is quite clear.

'Awakening' is the clearest understanding that the only reality is the Source, the Consciousness, and that the manifestation and its functioning that is called life is only a dream in this Universal Consciousness. Deliverance is the awareness – to be constantly aware – that daily living means dealing with each situation as one thinks fit, and that death brings about the end of this dream of life. Deliverance means accepting the spontaneity of daily living.

The flash of total acceptance, "I cannot be the doer of any deed" – that everything is a happening – is sudden. But, living one's daily life with this total sense of non-doership is gradual. To live as a man of understanding, totally spontaneously and naturally, without the slightest self-consciousness, may take time. Of course, the man of understanding is not concerned about this.

Getting the driver's licence is one thing. But being a seasoned driver, driving confidently through heavy traffic, may take some time. Until one day, you realise that you have just driven for one hour through heavy traffic without the least mental stress.

GOD AND RELIGION

Why does one believe in 'God'? Because it gives satisfaction, consolation, hope, and one says it gives significance to life. But what is meant by 'God'? Most people think of 'God' as an all-powerful entity, which God clearly is not. God can really mean only the Source, the only Reality. Neither the believer nor the non-believer will find God for the simple reason that Reality is the unknown. And one's belief or non-belief in the unknown is nothing more than a self-projection.

Yet, the people who say they believe in 'God' have destroyed a good part of the world and the world is in chaos.

The fundamental human problem is to understand the misery and confusion that exist within ourselves and, thus, in the world. Organised group thought – the basis of religion – being merely repetitive, cannot provide the solution.

The most important thing is to find clarity within ourselves. This clarity is not the outcome of mere cultivation of the intellect. Nor can it be conformity to pattern, however noble. This clarity can come about only through right thinking, and right thinking comes only with self-knowledge. Without self-knowledge, without understanding oneself, there is no basis for thought, for truth.

All organised beliefs are really based on separation, though they may preach brotherhood. It is only through creative understanding of ourselves that we can hope to have peace and harmony.

The key to this fundamental problem is the Gospel precept: "Judge not that you be not judged." This precept applies to all the ordinary man's dealings with others. Judgement will stop only when one is able to accept, totally, through one's own experience, what the Buddha has stated so positively: "Everything is a happening according to the Cosmic Law, and not any deed by an individual entity."

Only non-doership can prevent judgement, which results in guilt and shame for one's own actions and hatred and malice towards the 'other' for his actions. But it is essential that non-doership is accepted through personal experience and not as a mere concept. Ideas and beliefs never unify. They are separative, destructive, though they may bring momentary consolation.

To know That, which is immeasurable, which is not of time, the mind has to be free from time, free from thinking, free from all concepts about God – be a still mind. But the mind that is disciplined, controlled, shaped into a frame of stillness is not a still mind. *God is that which comes into being from moment to moment in a mental state of freedom and spontaneity – in the interval between two thoughts.*

The main point in this regard is that, as Lord Krishna has pointed out to Arjuna in the Bhagavad Gita (XI/32), everything in this universe is predetermined. And now, even some modern physicists and mathematicians, Stephen Hawking, for example, have accepted the concept of predetermination on a scientific basis.

Therefore, how can a prayer alter what is predetermined? Whether a prayer is answered or not – whether one gets what one has asked for – has already been decided. What role does prayer play in daily living? Prayer in daily living implies petition, supplication to what one might call 'God' being an all-powerful entity. Therefore, the approach is one of seeking a reward, a gratification. One is in trouble and prays for guidance or one is confused and prays for clarity.

I have sometimes wondered what I would say if, at any time,

God presented himself to me and offered me one wish. I would be expected to clearly say, in the simplest terms, what I wanted and I would have it.

I came to an answer: I would ask God to give me a state of mind in which I would want nothing from anyone, not even from Him.

There is also another point: How can Reality – God – answer one's particular demand? Can the Immeasurable be concerned with the petty little worries, miseries, and confusions of a three-dimensional object in the manifestation? Then again, a person praying for direction in a difficult situation may get an answer, but it can only be the response of the unconscious layers of his own mind that project themselves into the conscious – not the Real.

Throughout history, various prescriptions have been given on how to keep in touch with God while living one's life. Each one of them has been based on what the seeker is supposed to do, and has, therefore, ended in frustration. Or, there is the mistaken impression that, by following a particular prescription, one is indeed in constant touch with God.

What this produces, if not frustration, is pride in one's achievement. This is worse because, deep down, the individual knows that he is not in constant touch with God, and that he is deceiving himself – again frustration of a worse kind.

In almost every family there are some religious practices to be followed. Rituals based on certain scriptures, which are regarded as the word of God, and the disobedience, or rejection of which, is regarded as a sin. The fact of the matter is that what are regarded as scriptures today were written at one time by some human being, by some 'enlightened' person. When he spoke, or wrote the matter, he obviously had certain people in mind, to whom his words were addressed.

Being one with God is not something one can achieve. And this is the basic fact of life. Yet, if one feels that he would like to keep in constant touch with the Divine whilst doing whatever is necessary in one's daily living, I would assure him that this is possible.

The best way, according to me, is to be constantly, passively aware of the breathing process: breath going out, then naturally coming in, and going out again. This is not a deep breathing exercise. This practice will keep one in touch with the Divine.

It is only a genuine understanding that can bring about oneness with God. And this understanding is what the Buddha told us 2500 years ago: "Everything is a happening according to the Cosmic Law, and not any deed by an individual entity."

Therefore, one lives one's life accepting everything that happens, through every human body-mind organism, doing whatever one thinks one should do in any given situation, while never forgetting that whatever happens is not the doing by any individual entity – neither oneself nor the 'other'.

With this deep understanding, one's daily living becomes accepting everything without blaming anyone for anything – neither 'me' nor the 'other'.

This means that one lives one's life, necessarily accepting whatever happens from moment to moment – pain or pleasure – without carrying the burden of guilt and shame for one's action, nor hatred, jealousy, or envy towards anyone else for his actions. This means living one's life in peace with oneself and harmony with the 'other'. This is precisely what is meant by being 'one with God' while living one's life from day to day.

DEATH I

One should really consider the matter of what death means, not when one is ill or unbalanced, or very close to it, but when one is living with vitality, with health and energy, knowing the organism must necessarily wear out some day. In dealing with this question, one must consider it, not from the point of immortality, but from the point of view of eternity – that which is timeless – and that is Now.

The real question is: Can one die psychologically now, die to everything one has known – one's pleasure, one's attachment, and one's dependence – without trying to find ways and means of avoiding it? This means putting an end to that which has continuity. When one actually dies, one, obviously, has to end everything without any argument.

Therefore, when someone says he is afraid of death, how can he be afraid of something he does not know? The fear of death is, therefore, really the fear of losing something belonging to him. Fear of losing arises when one holds on to things that have given him or her satisfaction. Therefore, the fear of the 'unknown' is really the fear of losing the accumulated known.

Fear comes into being when one persists in being in a particular pattern, wanting to live in a certain frame. And any action to break the frame will only create another pattern. What is the basic frame, the pattern? There is only one answer: the mind itself is the frame, the pattern.

Why does the fear arise in the first place? Again, there is only one answer: because one is not able to accept the 'what-is'. One has had the experience of extraordinary freedom and joy at sometime or another. Why is the experience so rare? Because, usually the mind, not being able to accept the 'what-is', is always busy creating a fictitious 'what-should-be' and is always in fear of not reaching it.

When the body is perfectly healthy, there is a certain joy of well-being. Similarly, when the mind happens to be free of the bundle of reactions, responses, memories, hopes, and frustrations, then there is also an experience of joyous well-being. The point is that in this experience, the 'me', the bundle of conditioning, is not there.

One really must find out for oneself what it means to die. Then there is no fear, every day is a new day. The mind and the eyes see life as something totally new: *Eternity*. For this, one is advised to live a life now, today, in which there is an end to everything that one began – all the knowledge that one has gathered, which means all experiences, all memories, all hurts, and all compassion with others.

This means ending all that every day, so that the next day, the mind is fresh, young, and innocent. *In other words, one must die every day to everything that the mind has collected during the day.* Perhaps, in this there is 'love', totally new every moment, which indeed could be 'eternity'. Love is always new every moment, whereas pleasure is based on time and continuity.

It is necessary to make a clear distinction – perhaps subtle but important – between mourning for someone and reacting emotionally to the loss of a near relative or a dear friend. The reaction to the loss of someone close is a natural, biological reaction in the body-mind organism as grief.

Prolonged mourning, over a period, is involvement of the ego as a reaction to what is a natural biological reaction. In other words, while an emotional reaction is perfectly natural, an involvement is a matter of ignorance.

Man is not prepared to give up the relative 'me' so as to be the absolute 'I'. He wants the 'me', a phenomenal object, to become the absolute subject. It is like the case of the drowning man not prepared to let go the hoard of gold. He expects death as a temporary disintegration that would bring, for the 'me', unalloyed and perpetual joy and happiness.

What happens after death? One would obviously be in the same state one was in before life started in the womb. One would return to the Source; one would be home.

Now one knows what it means to 'die'. Now there is no fear. The body-mind organism has biological preferences, but there is no attachment – positive or negative – to any person or object.

There is no attachment to life itself. Therefore, there is no aversion to death either. Perhaps this is what is really meant by the word 'freedom'.

LIVE LIKE GOD

THE ONLY WAY TO LIVE I

A visitor told me that he would like to live according to the will of God, but his difficulty was he did not know the will of God. He was stunned when I told him that in any situation, he may do whatever he thinks he should do, and he could not go against God's Will.

What anyone does in a situation is based on what he wants and how he should get it. But having done whatever he wanted to do, what actually happens has never been in his control. In other words, he can do whatever he wants to do, according to his free will, but what actually happens will be according to God's Will.

Also, what one thinks is his 'free will' depends on two factors – his 'genes' and his 'conditioning', over neither of which did he have any control. It is God who determined his 'genes' and his 'conditioning'. Therefore, it is God who created the individual human being's 'free will'. How can anyone ever do what God does not want him to do? Good deeds, bad deeds – and their consequences – happen strictly according to God's Will.

This is the very basis of daily living and has always been truly simple.

One sees something and there is a biological reaction in the body-mind organism, positive or negative – anger or fear, or compassion, or whatever. Then, the ego promptly reacts to this biological reaction and identifies itself with it. In the case of the ordinary man, thinking comes in: "I was angry and I don't want to get angry. My doctor keeps telling me that frequent anger will raise my blood pressure..." This reaction to the biological reaction is an involvement of the ego in horizontal time, whether it is negative like anger or fear, or positive like compassion. And this involvement in the case of the ordinary person continues almost all day, situation after situation, resulting in physical strain and mental stress.

In the case of the man of understanding, what usually happens is that, with the understanding that everything is a happening according to God's Will or the Cosmic Law, and that the individual entity is powerless to do anything, the ego is totally free of any guilt and shame for any of his actions, and also free of any hatred towards anyone for the latter's action. The result is that the ego of the man of understanding, being totally free of any involvement, is open to the whole universe, open to any communion with the Source.

In any situation, the man of understanding is not tense, and is therefore never unaware of the fact that the Reality is one unity, that all the seemingly-different parts of the universe are manifestations of the one whole, united Reality.

This unity can actually be experienced in daily living. When the man of understanding is out in the open, sitting under a tree, enjoying the gentle breeze that is blowing, for instance, he does not let it pass by him. He lets it move within him and pass through his whole body. The rustling of the leaves as it passes through the branches of the tree is also felt by the man of understanding as his ego has not built a citadel around itself as a protection against the 'other', as is done by the ordinary man.

If the ego has not built this walled prison around one, it is possible to actually feel that one breathes not only through the nose, but through every pore of the body. Every cell of the body is a living organism and every cell is breathing. One can actually feel the oneness of the body with the whole of nature, if one is truly open to the universe.

When one hears something, one may think one is hearing through one's ears, but the fact is that one is hearing it through the whole of one's being. This is more easily felt when one is listening to some deep music, or to some words of deep meaning uttered by a genuine man of understanding, words coming out not just from the lips but from the very heart. When this kind of listening happens, the impact is fantastic, because the listening is happening through the entire being, without any barrier.

It is possible to live one's life fully and not fragmentarily, receiving only parts that one wants and rejecting others one does not like, as one ordinarily does. One has to be open to everything, and not only to concepts which appeal to one's existing conditioning. This is the key to real living. Live like God. Indeed, whatever one does at any time is precisely what God intends and expects one to accept – together with the consequences, which are also God's Will. To accept 'what-is', at any time, is to live like God.

Could it be that the only way to live is to live like God? One's apparent free will is determined by God. Everyone can only 'act' according to the Divine script. Therefore, one always does live like God, doing whatever one wants to do, based on genes and conditioning, which God has created.

THE RIGHT ATTITUDE TO LIFE I

The man of understanding begins his daily living like God and continues living like God for the rest of the day. Whereas, an ordinary person begins the day like God but, sometime during the day, reverts to living it out as the ordinary man when he or she blames another person for any happening. At the end of the day, one goes to bed like a human being, afraid of living and afraid of dying.

If every human being cannot help doing, at any moment, precisely what God wanted him to do, is he not living like God? The moment one says, "That is wrong, he should not have done this or she should not have done that," in that moment, God has left him and he has become just like any other human being.

Living like God, means living in the Now, living in the present moment:

1. Doing whatever one feels like doing in any situation – with total free will but no control over what happens thereafter.
2. Accepting that whatever happens thereafter is God's Will or the Cosmic Law and, therefore, enjoying the pleasure of the moment and suffering the pain, without blaming anyone: neither oneself nor the 'other'.
3. Living from moment to moment, without any regrets for the past, without any complaints about the present, and without any expectations of the future.

This way, the individual free will is still the very basis of the mechanism of daily living. Each individual is dealing with the existing situation, doing whatever he feels he should do according to his free will. Yet, whatever happens thereafter – the result and its consequences – has never been a matter of individual will: it is Cosmic Will.

The two are not contraries but complementaries which lead to natural spontaneity: accepting what happens, and the effect of each happening, as precisely what is supposed to happen according to God's Will, the Cosmic Law.

A tiny seed sprouts and grows into a tree, full of blossoms and fruits, in a natural progression. So is it with everything in the cosmos, including the human being. Not accepting the flow of life, comparing, judging, and condemning what happens is the human way of living life, which can only end in frustration and unhappiness.

Therefore, is it happiness:

When one has had a good meal or a satisfying sexual experience?

When one's team wins a cricket, hockey, or football match?

When one has passed a difficult exam?

When one has avenged an old insult?

When a severe migraine attack is finally over?

When one sees that one's friends are really enjoying themselves at one's party?

When one has laughed oneself silly during a funny movie?

When many people have paid one sincere compliments at a function?

When one is promoted as president of one's company?

One would probably be inclined to say that it is not happiness because whether it was joy or even ecstasy, it was only momentary, temporary – it did not last. And the same would apply to any experience, material or even spiritual; only joy, momentary.

One intuitively feels that what one is really looking for in life is something much deeper, which would transcend the pleasure or pain in the moment that is the essence of the flow of life. In other words, happiness cannot exist in the flow of life, over which no one can have any control, not even God if He is living His life in the role of a human being.

Therefore, happiness cannot exist in the flow of life but only in an attitude to life that would make one live one's life like God. This means accepting the predetermined pleasure or pain of the moment without any involvement and, therefore, without judging and condemning anyone – neither oneself nor the 'other' – so that one lives life in harmony with the 'other' (not 'me' versus the 'other') and in peace with oneself.

The life of Rama as a prince provides a typical example. Even as a prince, he had to have, like any other human being, his share of the usual pleasures and pains. He had to face the same problems and difficult decisions to make; perhaps the most difficult decision was when, according to the prevailing social and religious norms, he had to abandon his wife, Sita, in an ashram.

In spite of having to face life's usual problems, Rama has been described as 'Shantamurti' – the epitome of peace and equanimity. This shows that he had clearly seen that the ultimate happiness – fundamentally different from the pleasure of the moment, however intense – depends not on the flow of life, but one's attitude to life.

The poet sage Bhatruhari has said: "Enjoyment is always accompanied by the fear of misery, social position is always accompanied by the fear of a downfall, wealth by the fear of loss, honour by the fear of humiliation, power by the fear of foes, physical beauty by the fear of old age, scriptural condition by the fear of fresh opponents, virtue by the fear of seduction, life by the fear of death. All the things of the world pertaining to human beings are attended with fear. Renunciation alone eliminates fear."

Living like God, therefore, obviously means the total acceptance of the duality of opposites, which is the basis of 'life', with the total certainty and conviction that all existence is basically illusory. There is the beautiful description of that quantum jump from objectivity to subjectivity, from the facts of life to the deep attitude to life, given by Master Kao Jeng: "At that moment my doubts were suddenly broken up. I felt as if I had jumped out of a trap. All the puzzling Koans of the Masters and the Buddhas, all the different issues and events of both present and ancient times became transparently clear to me. Suddenly all things in life were settled; nothing under the Sun remained but peace."

The spontaneous way in which the man of understanding lives his life – like God – can be seen in various ways if one analyses the routine in which Rama must have lived his everyday life, like any other man of understanding. In his apparent actions, Rama must have acted according to the prevailing social regulations and legal provisions, but in his attitude to life as such, all his actions must have formed part of his effortless way of living.

The ordinary man who sees God as something separate from himself may have to meditate on the principle 'I am God'. But the man of understanding who has realised, totally, that God is all there is, that the 'me' and 'other' are both instruments through which God acts, has nothing to meditate upon. Therefore, Rama must have been content to do whatever he was expected to do in the particular circumstances, but was not really involved either in the doing of it or the non-doing of it. He was totally aware that all actions taking place through the body-mind organism are not really individual actions but happenings according to the Cosmic Law.

There are some who believe in the existence of the manifestation, yet others may believe that it does not exist, but Rama was not concerned with any such concepts and, therefore, was always serene, living life unruffled and unagitated, unlike the ordinary man.

KRISHNA SPEAKS I

> "*The Omnipresent Lord does not take note of the merit or demerit of anyone. What Is is always perfect. The light of the Atman is covered by the darkness of delusion, and that is how the human beings are deluded.*"
>
> – Bhagavad Gita, Chapter V/15

This verse firmly demolishes the concept of a God sitting somewhere in the clouds, peeping down and keeping a perfect account of every sin and every good deed done by every single human being, so that an individual may be punished or rewarded in due course. It should be clear that such a concept is steeped in ignorance. Such a concept cannot prevail if one is totally convinced that no action can happen except by God's Will. If God's Will is totally accepted, one's personal will cannot exist and, therefore, there cannot be any question of any sin or merit.

Such a concept is bound to evoke, immediately, an argument such as this: "If it is God's Will that I should commit a murder, why should I be punished for it?" The answer is astonishingly simple. There is no 'you' to be punished or rewarded; it was God's Will, and the destiny of that human organism, that the murder would be committed, and it is also God's Will, and the destiny of that organism, to be punished for the act.

> "It is indeed impossible for an embodied being to renounce action entirely, but he who has renounced the fruits of action is said to be truly non-attached."
> – Bhagavad Gita, Chapter XVIII/11

In this verse, Lord Krishna clearly brings out the difference between renunciation of action and renunciation of the fruits of action.

The word 'renunciation' usually means, for the average person, renouncing or giving up action. But giving up action is an impossibility because the energy within the organism will not allow the organism to remain idle for any length of time.

The one who is truly non-attached is the one who is not concerned with the fruits of action. And the ordinary person, fully identified with the organism as a separate entity with the independence of choice and action, would never be able to renounce the fruits of action and would, in all probability, consider himself entitled to the fruits of his action.

The only way the renunciation of the fruits of action can happen is when the deepest intuitive understanding happens that no action can ever be the individual's action, that all actions are, in fact, reactions of the body-mind organism to the outside impulse according to its natural characteristics.

> *"That knowledge is* sattvika *(pure) by which the one Imperishable Being, the deathless, is seen in all existences in the midst of all the diversity."*
> – Bhagavad Gita, Chapter XVIII/20

Seeing the Oneness, not only in the immense variety in the manifestation but also between the manifest and the unmanifest, is what is really meant by enlightenment or awakening.

Once the individual forgets this Oneness – not only between the manifestation as in its diversity, but also between the manifest and the unmanifest – he begins to think in terms of his individuality and his personal security. Once he begins to think in terms of personal security, he creates any number of problems for himself. So, at that level, the first step in understanding the nature of the human being would be that there can be no such thing as security for the individual, that movement and change are the very basis of life and living. This understanding is the basis of understanding life, to go back into the impersonality of life, in which the individual is merely an instrument.

Such understanding is 'sattvika' or pure knowledge.

> "I am come as Time, the ultimate eroder of the people, ready for the hour that ripens to their end. The warriors, arrayed in hostile armies facing each other, shall not live, whether you strike or stay your hand.
> Therefore, arise and fight. Win kingdom, wealth, and glory. Merely be the apparent instrument for their end – they have already been slain by Me – O, ambidextrous bowman."
> – Bhagavad Gita, Chapter XI/32, 33

Everything that is born or created must end – this is the law of nature, and in the process, human beings become the apparent reasons and instruments. In fact, they have nothing to do other than being mere instruments. They have no free will or choice. In this verse, Lord Krishna tells Arjuna that although Arjuna thinks in terms of himself being the killer and the enemies being the ones he would kill, actually he, as Time, has already killed them. There is no need for Arjuna to feel any regret. Arjuna's unhappiness stems from his feeling of personal doership, and here again, the Lord reminds Arjuna that he can never be anything but an apparent instrument for whatever happens as part of the functioning of Totality. In subtle terms, the Lord tells Arjuna not to question the functioning of Totality, to enjoy the 'kingdom, wealth, and glory' that is his destiny – never forgetting that these too will be subject to the ultimate demolition and annihilation due to the efflux of Time.

In the Mahabharata, we can clearly see how Lord Krishna lived his life like an ordinary mortal, and it makes the most interesting reading:

1. As a child, he could be naughty and irritate mother Yashoda like any other child.
2. As an adult he was concerned with the lives of many others in both the Kaurava family and the Pandava family, the opponents in the famous Mahabharata war, in each situation doing whatever he felt he should do.
3. When both Duryodhana and his cousin Arjuna went to him for help in their war, he offered them the choice: His entire army on the one side, and he himself, without taking part in the fighting, on the other. Promptly, Duryodhana chose to have the army, and Arjuna preferred to have Lord Krishna.

4. When Draupadi, as the princess, was to be married, there was, according to the custom of the day, an extremely difficult competition to which all the royal princes were invited. When Karna approached the competition ring, he cut such an impressive figure that the princess promptly lost her heart to the magnificent Karna, but it was Lord Krishna who exposed Karna as being ineligible to compete, knowing full well that he could have easily won. He wanted Draupadi to wed Arjuna. He did what he felt he should do in the situation.
5. Much later, when Karna lay dying on the battlefield, Lord Krishna quickly responded to Karna's request that he should light the funeral pyre. Lord Krishna was fully aware of the many wonderful qualities of Karna, particularly his generosity.
6. In the mace duel between prince Duryodhana and Bhima, it was Lord Krishna who persuaded Bhima, much against his will, to hit an unethical blow below the belt, and kill Duryodhana.
7. Later, when the Kauravas were defeated, the mother of the Kaurava princes, knowing that it was Krishna who was primarily responsible for the destruction of her family, put a curse of destruction on the whole Yadava clan, to which he belonged, for what Krishna had done.

Krishna, with his deep understanding, knew he would have to accept the consequences as part of what was predetermined according to the Cosmic Law.

The entire life of Lord Krishna as a human being shows that he acted, in any situation, precisely according to his free will, but that all consequences would necessarily have to be according to what was predetermined according to the Cosmic Law, and have to be accepted. Lord Krishna shows us how to live like God.

Living like God means living life spontaneously, accepting everything as a happening and not the doing of any individual entity; this means, in other words, not judging or condemning anyone for any action, although, of course, society will continue to judge all actions according to social regulations and legal provisions.

Finally, living like God means never pursuing any desire, while certainly enjoying all desires whenever they are satisfied, content with one's lot in life, going wherever life takes one, unmindful of where one happens to be at the end of the day – and the end of his or her designated life span.

Note: The Kauravas and Pandavas were two clans, of the Kuru dynasty, who fought one another in the Mahabharata war. Arjuna, the third son of Pandu and Kunti, led the Pandavas in the war. Duryodhana, the eldest son of King Dhritarashtra and Gandhari of Hastinapur, led the Kauravas. Draupadi was the daughter of King Drupada of Panchala. Bhima was the elder brother of Arjuna. Karna was the illegitimate son of Kunti.

THE ONE ESSENCE

Not to be able to accept the very basis of life and living – the uncertainty in life – means perpetual frustration. Neither the man of understanding nor the ordinary person can avoid the pain or the pleasure, which the moment will bring.

'Acceptance of what-is' does not mean not doing whatever one feels one should do in the circumstances. 'Acceptance' includes doing whatever one feels one should do in a particular situation. Otherwise, this acceptance would be a restricted one, a forced one.

The most important point about 'acceptance of what-is' is the fact that the acceptance in any situation must include not only the absence of resentment against anyone, but the total acceptance that in any situation, what has happened is a happening according to the Cosmic Law, and not the doing by any individual.

The whole point is that if a happening is not the doing of any individual entity, no one can be blamed for it – neither oneself nor the 'other'. Therefore, importantly, there can never be any guilt or shame for oneself, or any hatred towards the 'other', whatever the effect of the happening, according to the Cosmic Law.

And, the absence of guilt and shame, and the absence of hatred for anyone, means the presence of peace of mind and a harmonious relationship with the 'other'. This is what every human being ultimately seeks in life.

It is because the ordinary man constantly chooses to accept or reject that he does not see the true nature of things: like a vast space where nothing is in excess and nothing is lacking, both counterparts of every conceivable kind are present.

Therefore, for every human being, acceptance of the present moment means: "I accept 'what-is' at the moment, precisely as it is, as something which is supposed to be according to God's Will or the Cosmic Law. And, while accepting the 'what-is', I do precisely what I think I should do in that situation, with the total acceptance that what actually happens has never been in my control, a fact which I must necessarily accept, together with the consequences."

The important point is that 'acceptance of what-is' means acceptance without any regrets of the past, without any complaints about the present, and without any expectations of the future.

Erroneous concepts will disappear by themselves when one is serene in the Oneness of things. When one tries to stop activity to achieve passivity, the very effort becomes activity.

One need not search for the truth but only stop conceptualising and creating opinions.

When the mind has accepted, totally, that everything is a happening according to the Cosmic Law – and not the deed done by anyone – nothing in the world can offend. The 'me' and the 'other' both become helpless instruments, through which happenings happen. One does whatever one thinks one should do in any situation.

When conceptualising ceases, the old mind ceases to exist; when 'thought – objects' vanish, the 'thinking mind – subject' also vanishes. If one does not discriminate between the two, one realises the mind of emptiness.

Thinking and attachment are the only real problems. Why be attached, even to the idea of enlightenment, and go astray? *Let life flow.*

One will go with the flow of life and walk freely and

undisturbed, if he follows the programming – genes and conditioning – working by itself without the burdensome practice of judging, which can only bring frustration and weariness.

Enlightenment simply means 'acceptance of what-is' including the world of senses. The man of understanding does not strive for any goals while the ordinary man fills himself with efforts and goals, distinctions, and discriminations. Enlightenment means the abolishing of all thinking like right and wrong, gain or loss.

If the mind stops making discriminations, liking and disliking, the million things are as they are – of single essence. To accept the One Essence is to be freed from all entanglements.

Being in the timeless self-essence without pride, guilt, and hatred, one enjoys true freedom. All self-centred striving ceases, there is neither 'me' nor the 'other', neither being nor non-being, neither perfection nor non-perfection. This is total freedom – self-realisation – in daily living.

In essence, "Who am I?"

The answer lies only in the understanding that this life and living is only a great dream, in which all human beings are thrown in as characters. We are really dreamers who are merely witnessing the functioning of the manifestation, 'life' as we know it.

"I am not the one who thinks he does the thinking, does the doing, and does the experiencing. I am the One who witnesses the thinking, the doing, the experiencing that is happening."

This is the final truth in daily living.

But the answer must come from personal experience.

Yet, I suggest a formula for daily living: humility within and tolerance for the 'other', contentment within and compassion for the 'other', not as something to be pursued, but as something that arises as a natural result of the understanding that everything is a happening according to the Cosmic Law, for which no one is to blame, neither oneself nor the 'other'.

This concept works in life because it is based on logic and universal experience: everything is a happening based on the Cosmic Law. How and whom it affects is, again, according to the Cosmic Law. No one does anything and therefore, no one can be blamed or condemned for anything. But each one has to live his life, doing whatever he thinks he is doing at any moment, accepting society's decision about every simple act – reward and punishment. And, therefore, pleasure or pain from moment to moment. This is daily living, over which one has no control.

It is in daily living that the human being expects to have

'happiness'. And he gets it if he is able to accept this concept totally because, then, the pleasure in the moment is not accompanied by pride in the ego, nor is pain accompanied by guilt for oneself or hatred for the 'other'. The absence of pride, of guilt, and of hatred for the 'other' means the presence of deep peace and happiness.

In the simplest of terms, this means living one's life without ever being uncomfortable with oneself at any moment.

In other words, living like Krishna.

THE FINAL PRAYER

O Lord,
give me
a state of mind
so filled with
Your Being
that I would not
need anything
from anybody,
anymore.
Not even
from You.

AFTERWORD I

Standing barefoot on the cool marble as the early morning light bathed its gold-plated dome, minarets, and outer walls in a luminous glow, I found myself totally at peace in the courtyard of the Golden Temple at Amritsar, in Punjab.

As the sun rose, its rays ricocheted off the gold-plated walls in a blaze of light that enveloped the entire Temple. Shimmering in the middle of the pond (sar) of nectar (amrit), which gives the city its name, the Golden Temple is the holiest shrine of the Sikh faith. However, its true beauty lies in the absence of any idol worship for there simply is *no* idol to worship. An ordinary visitor, with no historical or cultural background of Sikhism, upon entering the inner sanctum, would perhaps be astounded to see devout pilgrims bowing down, or even prostrating themselves, before a jewel-encrusted marble platform upon which rests what appears to be a large book wrapped in a pink cloth.

This object of devotion is the *Guru Granth Sahib* – the holiest book of the Sikhs.

The *Guru Granth Sahib* is a compilation of devotional prayers, hymns, and poems composed by the ten Sikh Gurus. A large part of it also includes compositions of various Hindu and Muslim saints and poets, thereby affirming the basic unity and 'One Essence' of all religions. It presents a perfect set of values and a practical code of conduct for every person. Rather than any living person, or one long gone, this Book is, indeed, the complete teacher and is revered as the 'living' guru of the Sikhs.

The true value of any teaching lies in its relevance to daily living – in the way it helps us face our situations, both the pleasures and pains that the flow of life brings – with equanimity. For, spiritual seeking should not just be confined to the study of ancient scriptures and lofty, philosophic ideals – it must also teach us how to apply what one has learnt to one's daily living.

A good example of a down-to-earth, practical approach vs. a theoretical one is put forward by Ramesh Balsekar when he says, "Of what use are big words like Enlightenment or

Self-realisation, unless we know exactly what it will give us in our daily living, which we did not have before Enlightenment?"

It is in this vein that Ramesh presents, with great simplicity and clarity, the Indian philosophy of Advaita (non-duality). "Its understanding," he says, "may not make one's life easier, but it would certainly help make life simpler."

May this book and the teaching contained in it, gift you the strength and courage displayed by Mother Teresa, when, with her sardonic wit, she remarked, "I know God will not give me anything I can't handle. I just wish He didn't trust me so much!"

In closing, I wish to thank Chris Andrelang for his patience and perseverance in giving form to this book, and for graciously accepting my suggestions and requests while he was editing the text.

– Gautam Sachdeva
March 2006

OTHER RAMESH BALSEKAR TITLES
PUBLISHED BY YOGI IMPRESSIONS

The Ramesh Balsekar Collector's Set (2010)

The End of Duality (2009)

Advaita on Zen and Tao (2008)

90 Steps to Oneness – Wisdom Deck (2007)

The Only Way to Live (2006)

Let Life Flow (2005)

The One in the Mirror (2004)

The Seeking (2004)

The Happening of a Guru: A Biography (2003)

Peace and Harmony in Daily Living (2003)

The Ultimate Understanding (2001)

Ramesh S. Balsekar (1917-2009), authored over 25 books in which he discussed the Indian philosophy of Advaita or Non-duality. The basic concept of his teaching was that "all there is, is Consciousness;" all actions are happenings, the functioning of the Primal Energy, and not the doing by anyone. Ramesh framed his concepts in the context of daily living, speaking from his experience as a bank president and a family man.

For information on Ramesh Balsekar visit:
www.rameshbalsekar.com

For further details, contact:
Yogi Impressions Books Pvt. Ltd.
1711, Centre 1, World Trade Centre,
Cuffe Parade, Mumbai 400 005, India.

Fill in the Mailing List form on our website
and receive, via email, information on
books, authors, events and more.
Visit: www.yogiimpressions.com

Telephone: (022) 61541500, 61541541
Fax: (022) 61541542
E-mail: yogi@yogiimpressions.com

 Join us on Facebook:
www.facebook.com/yogiimpressions

ALSO PUBLISHED BY YOGI IMPRESSIONS

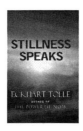   

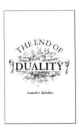 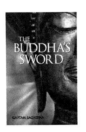  

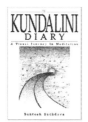

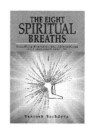

DVDs

AUDIO CDs

Create greater balance and wholeness within yourself with

Contemporary High-Tech Meditation® Audio CDs

Brought to you by:

When meditation was first conceived thousands of years ago, its techniques were suited for a simple, very different way of life. Today, we live in a chaotic, high-stress environment where time, calm and clarity can be elusive.

The Synchronicity Experience: quite simply, it meditates you
Its proprietary Holodynamic® Vibrational Entrainment Technology (HVET) developed by its Founder, Master Charles Cannon, is embedded in musical meditation soundtracks that literally meditate you while you listen.

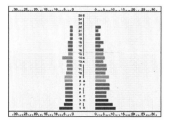

Brain monitor of a typical non-meditator shows pronounced hemispheric imbalance and fragmented, limited brain function.

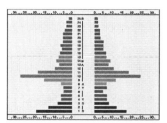

A regular user of Synchronicity Contemporary High-Tech Meditation® develops a high degree of synchronization indicating whole brain function.

Taking the guesswork and randomness out of the meditative process, the meditation soundtracks are available in the Alpha and Theta formats for light and medium meditation. Whether you are an experienced meditator or just starting to meditate, our CDs will help deliver a four-fold increase in results compared to traditional methods.

Om   Om Namah Shivaya   Harmonic Coherence   Welcome To My World   Om Mani Padme Hum

Sounds Of Source Vol. 1-5   Time Off   Song Of The Ecstatic   Romancing The Moment – The Love Meditation   Blessed Mother A Thousand Names

Hear the Audio Clips on our website: www.yogiimpressions.com